DUANE LOCKE

THE FIRST DECADE
(1968-1978)

edited by Alan Britt & Paul B. Roth

BITTER OLEANDER
P R E S S

2012

The Bitter Oleander Press
4983 Tall Oaks Drive
Fayetteville, New York 13066-9776 USA

www.bitteroleander.com
info@bitteroleander.com

First Edition

ISBN# 0-9786335-7-1

Library of Congress Control Number: 2012930852

Cover Design and Layout: *Roderick Martinez*
Compiled and edited by *Paul B. Roth*

Cover Painting: *The Past Believing in the Future Becomes a Present Becoming a Now*
            by Duane Locke

Printed by McNaughton & Gunn, Inc.
Saline, Michigan 48176-0010
www.bookprinters.com

Distributed in the United States by Small Press Distribution, Inc.
Berkeley, CA 94710-1409
www.spdbooks.org

Manufactured in the United States of America

ACKNOWLEDGMENTS

Grateful acknowledgment must be paid those journals in which most of these poems first appeared:

South Florida Review, Poetry Florida, Ann Arbor Review, Human Voice Quarterly, Roundtable, Quince, Premiere, The Other, Euphoria (England), Black Sun, Mimeo, Grafitti, Love, Avalanche, From the Other Side of Silence, Intermission, Midwestern University Quarterly, Southern Poetry Review, Lampeter Muse, Poet Lore, Wormwood Review, Stolen Paper Review, Forum, dust, Athene, Magazine, Motive, Ball State University, Epos, Nexus, Tangent, Fine Arts Discovery, Poetry Bag, Poetry Newsletter, Cape Rock Quarterly, Olé, Camels Coming, Volume 63, Dasein, Today, Oyez!, Perspectives, Abraxas, Eikon, Blitz, Micromegas, Roanoke Review, Corduroy, Steppenwolf, Manhattan Review, Gnosis, Folio, Suction, Panama Gold and Beacon Press for its publication of "Beetle" in *For Neruda, For Chile*

and to those presses from whose books the following selections were made:

Inland Oceans (The Beanbag Press, 1968), *From the Bottom of the Sea* (Black Sun Press, 1968), *Dead Cities* (Gunrunner Press, 1969), *Lightbulbs' Lengthened Eyelashes and Storks' Nests* (Ghost Dance Press, 1969), *Rainbows Under Boards* (University of Tampa Review Press, 1969), *The Submerged Fern in the Waistline of Solitude* (Ann Arbor Review Press, 1972), *Immanentist Sutras* (Ann Arbor Review Press, 1973), *The Poems of Duane Locke* (UT Review Press, 1974), *The Various Light* (UT Review Press, 1975), *Foam on Gulf Shore* (UT Review Press, 1978)

CONTENTS

DEAD CITIES (1969)

LIGHTBULB'S LENGTHENED EYELASHES AND STORK NESTS (1969)

RAINBOWS UNDER BOARDS *(1969)*

THE SUBMERGED FERN IN THE WAISTLINE OF SOLITUDE *(1972)*

IMMANENTIST SUTRAS (1973)

THE POEMS OF DUANE LOCKE (1974)

THE VARIOUS LIGHT (1975)

FOAM ON GULF SHORE (1978)

DUANE LOCKE

THE FIRST DECADE
(1968-1978)

HEIGHTENED SENSE OF REALITY:
DUANE LOCKE'S FIRST DECADE

Duane Locke wrote his first poems on a dare. Engaged in friendly publishing competition with a colleague, Locke was asked by Fred Wolven when, how and why his first poems were written. Locke responded: *It was January, 1962. I was encouraged by the poet David Wade...I was engaged on a scholarly work on seventeenth century poetry (Donne to Marvell), relating modes of perception as manifest in the imagery to the influences of different medieval philosophies. I decided to give it up and start on poems.* His earliest poems attracted immediate attention. In fact, his first poem "Kissing a Mechanical Ape" was selected for the influential anthology *Southern Writing in the Sixties* published by Louisiana State University Press. A painter and renowned nature photographer by the time he discovered the joy of writing poems, Locke had already cultivated the keen sense of observation that would pervade his later poetry.

Similar to Neruda who once suggested that poems seemed to leap from his skin, poems exploded from Locke's blazing imagination: *My poems were exorcisms...*Locke explained...*spells to cast out the evils that daily threatened to destroy our inwardness and humanity.* Folks were immediately attracted. Poets, editors and students alike were mesmerized by Locke's ability to write with clarity, depth and originality. What others found challenging to express, Locke seemed to clarify with ease in poems about *the debasement of life by the dominant values of the established order* to subjects that exalted him: *goldfinches, herons, katydids, hermit crabs* and *ferns.* But unlike other poets with unique sensibilities, Locke did more than clarify what so many struggled to express. Locke's unique blend of careful observation with concrete particularized imagery sparked new connections in the brain, excited neurons which were dormant or had been dulled to sleep by a culture content to turn its citizens into robotrons fueling the industrial machine.

The latter half of the 1960's and first half of the 1970's was a revolutionary period in American art and culture. Though he would never subscribe to it, Locke's poems were torches for the times that burned with the clarity of magnesium while illuminating the frailty of the human condition, thus creating a new sensibility, a fresh awareness enabling people to navigate the lack of fulfillment in their lives. In fact Locke's appeal was so strong that during his first poetic decade he became the most published poet in America. Being an extremely prolific poet helped but writing one remarkable poem after another helped even more. The late Hugh Fox once expressed amazement at Locke's ability to achieve such a high level with every poem while adding that Locke's *rhythms are elliptical, staccato, condensed, the symbol-packages float by with surrealistically subjective (but never objective) connections...Which explains the cage of finches in the tropical Tampa backyard, the isolated book-lined room above the garage in a separate building in back of the house, filled with pictures of egrets and ibises and herons, or Mrs. Locke telling me how much they liked to find sand where their footprints were the only ones, and where there were still birds.*

So it is not surprising that around this time young poets flocked to Locke like lost ships to a beacon. Inside a handful of years Locke inspired so many students to write and publish that without intending to he created what became known as the Tampa School of Poetry, later the Linguistic Realists and still later the Immanentists. When asked about his inspired young flock, Locke offered: *In three years my classes in creative writing have produced thirty-one poets who have published nationally (this was Steve Barfield's count).* Special issues of journals featured Locke and his young Immanentists followed by anthologies of immanentist poetry. The movement generated much attention in America and in Europe where the great French poet Yves Bonnefoy once praised the Immanentists as the most exciting poets to emerge from America in generations.

Well, decades passed as decades do, and Duane Locke at a robust 90 years of age continues to write at an astounding rate. A few years ago he pioneered poetry on the Web and as of this introduction has published over 6,500 poems in print and on the Web. He continues to photograph blue egrets, snakes, spiders and beetles in his lusty Florida environment and knocks out the occasional dozen paintings or so whenever he gets the urge. One of Locke's first publishers Fred Wolven said years ago: *Duane Locke is a classic example of a writer who successfully utilizes knowledge as a noted amateur nature photographer and a Renaissance scholar in establishing his mark as a contemporary poet...Photos, images, surrealistic effects, and mythical imagination are all garnered by Duane Locke to express a heightened sense of reality in order to present a twentieth-century vision — a vision of man's existence.*

Alan Britt
Towson University
January 2012

THE FIRST DECADE

(1968-1978)

*for Helen and Jack Dayan,
whose friendship makes life worth living.*

KISSING A MECHANICAL APE

On the side street near the discount house, I saw
a man of marriageable age kissing a mechanical ape.
Then this same man began hugging himself.
I asked, "What does this mean?"
He replied, "I refuse to destroy my emblem by reasoned discourse,"
and he continued to hug himself.
This is a strange neighborhood, I thought,
I am returning to main street where there are traditional stores.
When I arrived each store was having a founder's day sale,
and I saw a thousand men in silkish suits,
each man hugging himself, and in silkish dresses
a thousand women each hugging their children.

1962

INLAND OCEANS

CACTUS

Cactus, old water hose
melted from neglect, leaning
on thirst, trying to find
a solar system without ice.
Cactus, keep curling
around my bones, and telling
me you are a speaking snake
brought from the Amazon
and escaped from a hencoop.
Tell me all that you want
is in my notebook, and you have
recopied the passages
that were erased by the streetlight.
Tell me that the Eskimo
will never touch you with a spear,
and the wearers of tie clips
will not put you in a can.
Let us praise our dry place,
and not run away into
the rain of alcohol
that falls from the bitten nails
of those who refuse
to search shadows. Let us
find in the sandgrains
a memory of the holy feathers
from the flown bird.
We can wait together in our labyrinth
until from Ariadne's grave the armadillo
brings an armful of thread.

CORAL CITIES

the movement toward coral cities, to see,
not to blink, not to turn away, not
to call for the chalk marks across a blackboard,
not to ask for the bones in the archeologist's
frozen street, not to step into the daydream's
infinite acts, but to see, to know what
is in the hand of the child standing by
the slaughtered buffalo, to compare the present hand
with the hand of smoke arising from the old teeth
piled in forgotten desk drawers, to forgo
the cosmological gardens that are given
to sleepers behind the barbed wire, to
twist out from the moment of idols, to move
toward the entrances of coral cities,
where the skeletons of animals
build apartments for the living.

CENTURIES HAD BROUGHT US

Centuries had brought us to camp
on the swamp's edge. Some of us
suspected the swamp was breathing,
but our leader following the movie reels
put his ear to the moss-covered earth,
and said he heard nothing but the soft tap
of a chorus girl's barefoot. He had
been trained by alligator hunters and men
who owned one thousand watt candelabras;
he moved with the immaculate precision
of a funeral parlor director.
When daylight came we were to follow
the trail chopped by old mens' unbuilt lives.
They had constructed the pathway
from tranquillizing lies about bedsteads.
Often we thought we saw a broken javelin
near a large fern, but our leader said
there was neither javelin n`or fern,
for us to read our instruction guide
and to stop staring into darkness.
We read that we were not to look at
the black spots on leaves, and never
to touch fallen pine needles or rotten wood.
We were always to hang-up on the gum tree's
telephone call, and if we obeyed
we would be given the phone numbers
of the new theologies that rock
at the top of the stairways to peeling paint hotels.
Most were satisfied by this promise,
and pulled the straps tight for the night,
but some of us were uneasy in our sleeping bags.

OUT FROM THE COLD CORNER

Out from the cold corner
Out from the meeting place of indifferent strangers
Out from cemeteries built by children in small rooms
Out from the firewatcher's tower crowded with color slides of smoke

The white moth
depositing the secret
on the midnight leaf

Thoughts of lemons that grow out of air
and vanish
when the branch of the lemon tree cannot be found
the tree that leans by an empty coffee cup in a lost backyard

At the desk with the secret humming in the dark tree
terror tapping in the desk drawer

Thoughts of all the eyes closed before the birth of the strawberry

Thoughts that somewhere
under the oak
an Indian pipe
is breaking through black dirt
and the Indian pipe is unseen

Thoughts of words carried by old families to the dwelling place
of the toothless comb

Thoughts of the pyramid's fatigue when the slaves sleep

Still the humming
Still the thoughts
Then the words spoken in ink
The caused caused
and a telology beyond a broken telephone

Then the secret flies from the leaf
and blushes in its nakedness
The written word seeks its axis
in another
Toward an understanding that eludes
the hardware department's pipe clamps

And forgetfulness covers the eyes of all the books
that stare from the bookends with the old rabbis

OUT THE DOOR

Out the door
Out the never to be opened door
Through the climate of steel
Through the streets where the metal dice
have eaten away
the curls of balconies

To the dissolution in the absolution of life's sea
The casting off of the skin unkissed by the snake
The casting off

To become all eyes
All wings
All eyes winged

The movement toward the flight inside the tree
Circling in circles
Circling in each circles' darkness
Circling in darkness to a strange light
a light untouchable and pure wood

Away from the required daily smile
Away from words spoken among evil chairs
Away from the black windows
that deny sainthood to the black widow spider

Away from the drunken bricklayer pushing
a wheelbarrow filled with white hair

In the tree
In all the affirmation and doubt of the tree
In the tree

THE DOCUMENTS THAT DEFEND
THE PENDULUM

The documents that defend the pendulum are burning
There is a birth
when the green skeletons under the weapons
are touched
There is a birth
when the basements of tears
are poured over the outstretched hands
There is a birth
when the litigations are exposed
as false rapture
An emergence from the steel egg
An emergence from the concrete cocoon
An emergence from the words
spoken on the fallen porch
A leap over the wall
of the arms
that cannot believe in trees
A leap beyond the sky
where the old minute moans
with a paralyzed tongue
The ferns kiss
The bamboos kiss
The weeds kiss

A VISION OF A BEGINNING

the empty frontiersman, a wound in his wheels,
opaque eyes
putting hinges
on angels
to stop the quiver in his piston hand,
counting Indian skulls,
putting labels on powder burns,
imprisoning women in long heavy dresses,
a sadist
frocked in a history book
and followed by centuries
of petty men
who spread fur and feathers on cement,
destroyer of redwoods,
destroyer of limpkins,
destroyer of a naked girl
arising from a murex shell.
He rushes toward the sea
to clothe her in the graffiti
gathered from carvings
on smokey mountain trees.

THE GREYBOARD HOUSE

After the signs
and the highway
the stop
but there was
not even the hum
I imagined to be
above the flower
in front of
the greyboard house
that had just
switched off
its lights forever.

EXCURSION

From the park's obsolete benches,
the curved iron,
the empty spaces between green boards,
the omnipresent pigeons,
and a young willow tree,
new leaves after winter,

a glance toward the hill,
a white building,
made of sand,
a faceless face in a
circle of gold,
knees touching antique bricks
and putting a face
on the faded.
Newspapers are not
needed, for the murder
occurred on
phantom mountain
and blossomed in tiny buds
before and under footsteps.
Their crows are old.

The children in this city
are not children,
for childhood is not allowed
among the bread crumbs
stolen from sparrows.

Nearby the movie lines,
the seeking of the
untouched marvelous.
I cannot give them
anything,
for they have seen
raw silver, and still

pour their daylight
into hungry sands.
I cannot give anything
only take away
a language
with an alphabet
of stone and cacti.

Down the street
the slaughter of the bull,
each face drinking
its cup of regimented blood
that will grow lace
around the collar
of a guitar night.
You cannot give me
anything,
but only take away
the sleep of sounds.

Tomorrow I cross
the rumored river.

IT IS NOT DEATH

It is not death
digging its way
up through the ground,
but a plant
that is not a vegetable,
but a stringless piano
played by
the ring fingers
of the dead
who built towers
above the mosquitos,
who caught the sand
and made bowels,
who rode over grasses
to a pavillion,
who carved their names
on liquors poured
from silk skirts.

It is not death
digging its way
up through the ground,
but a music
that never waits
for a door,
a music that enters
from the lips
of newspapers,
a music that comes
from the lightbulb
flashing from the bones
of the eaten gazelle,
a music that is
polished by highways,
a music that is hidden
by tobacco planters

under the steeples of sleep,
a music that wraps the fingers
in autombile fenders
and sends touch
to the trigger
of a revolver.

FROM THE BOTTOM
OF THE SEA

THE FOOT TRACKS OF THE BIRD

A sculptural language that has not the sound of the chisel
but the foot tracks of birds,
scratches in leaves,
sunken darkness on damp sand,
wet silence on river rocks,
not the chisel's tapping,
not the drum, not the tympani's low notes
for old men standing by the missing staircase,
the old men on newspaper beds,
the old men who have dreamed of herding thousands
of bulls into boxcars—
they cannot sleep by a broken fence.
Only the skeletons of hummingbirds enter the old men's dreams,
not the rubythroat not the greencrown not the blackchin,
not the forest hidden in the feathers.
The old men press
their lips to knife scars.

Images have many hands
and grab what is not seen in the reaching,
but seen only by the gold eyes carried by bees
to the red crossroads of the hibiscus.

Words from sparrows nesting in the eaves of asphalt lunch rooms,
not vagueness or obscurity,
not the mist that softens the steel prongs of the eyelash
that winks in accord with the drum,
not the night-light darkness carried in each man's phrases,
not the meaninglessness of the colloquial vocabulary discussing love,
but a language sculptured by the foot tracks of birds,
with a patina brought by the songs of birds,
the ani the owl the whippoorwill the flycatcher
the rattle in the rusty pulley belt of the hummingbird's voice.

THE LEAF

the beginning comes not from the bag on the antique desk,
not from falling into the soft nets of many hands.

the beginning comes from the microscope of the eye,
from the brain's focusing on the leaf,
the brown and green leaf, the long leaf,
the spear shaped leaf, the wavering leaf,
the leaf surrounded by ripples of frog water,
the leaf floating over a field of slaughtered cows,
the leaf bleeding into eternity,
the leaf sharing the tears falling
from the giraffe fingers of stunted hands,
the leaf covering the hand with green circles.

UNSEENS

This is not a tent but it has flaps not closed that can be closed
Wind or words or hope or despair hold the unseen against the unseen
But this unseen is not the unseen that puts my speech into the banana
    blossom
This unseen is that which hangs around the necks of those who shot
    night from the sky
It is the unseen in the tones of the picture that never knew the sorrows
    of broken glass
It is the unseen that plays a drum in the high-priced underground of
    pitchmen
This is the unseen that holds the flaps of what is not a tent open
There is another unseen that sleeps in the pepper bush

A SOLILOQUY AT THE BEGINNING
OF SUMMER

A lion   a sheep   a goat   a heifer

a vegetable in the mist
a vegetable in the fog
a vegetable in the sea
and a fig tree

a rock   a stone   a pebble
pyrites and quartz

From this the visible to this the invisible

Leave to himself the man biting the lettuce leaf
go away to a closet
to talk with the lettuce plant

No knowledge except on the ledges of waterfalls
No knowledge in the ink sketches made in biology class

Honorius of Autun: "Every Creature
is a shadow of truth and life."

Not in the outward
Not in the bones on the tray
Not in the counting and cataloguing of nerves

Only in the inward
hidden from invitations by iron doors
hidden from hands in long gloves
hidden from the kneelers before stopped-up sinks

A bird
a black and white bird
an upside down bird
upside down on an air plant
speaks out of silence

speaks beyond the wrapping paper from antique cities
and all that is invisible becomes invisible

I turn away from those who
talk without speaking
who wear false water in their eyes
who assert strongly
but assert only
their death

Not in the study of things
but in the inner meaning of things
that have no meaning beyond themselves

I shall leave those who can never kneel
before the unmined tin in the mountain
and shall worship the words spoken
by the voices
the sky   the water   the trees
and the symmetry of all bent things

AFTER READING A NEWSPAPER

Bulls escape from slaughter pen,
disturb a neighborhood.

I stare through their happy eyes.
Nibble on garden roses.

ROOTS

The bank I stand on
is bright with the damp language
of roots.
Voices under my feet
are mingled in the mud
with echoes
from a system of snails.

THE GULF

Bulldozers of an indifferent green,
their salt fingernails filled with death,
crush and claw the sand,
sending up the vacated houses
of evicted snails
to crumble on the defrocked roots of pines.
The lumber of the small white pier trembles
and shakes a bucket of minnows into the lecturing waves.

THE HEDONIST

I never received much pleasure
from doing the forbidden:
sneaking a smoke behind the lunch room,
stealing milk bottles from the irate grocer.
I never received much pleasure
from doing the approved:
beating up the neurotic and perverted,
breaking Easter lilies in the whore's backyard.
My teacher, to put me wise,
told me that I was selfish,
thought only of myself,
and if I did not change,
would grow up to be very lonely.

MEDITATION OF ACHILLES

We go to a strange land
to play the games of blood.

The fuel in our home heaters
has a dull smell,
and we must set some distant straw afire.

There is a mocker in the public square
who crawls through the windows of a leaf.
He must be hung
if our dead fathers are going to live.

POLLUTION

Ferns' shadows cross the sky's
reflection falling between cypress trees.

My legs sink up to the knees
in the thick black water;
I watch the seeds gather around.

I stand in a circle of future trees,
and wait for the ferns to call.

But they speak only to the frogs.
I look at my hands,
creased with traffic lights,
stare at the regimen of red and green.

THE HOUSE WITHOUT SHUTTERS

The two-fisted house without shutters
lets the streets in,
and the grey-templed windows
tell us to trust
the voice of street corners.

The room corners of contemplation
are blocked by marble faces
speaking antique mottoes, and there is
no place to stand except in the middle
where the floor is street noise.

All the aged whispers tell us
to abandon our hesitations, open
our enclosures, let the winds' children
whisper the stories of the street.

We pause in the shivers of our empty hands,
but we stubbornly inquire:
what and where are these voices.
The angry house refuses to listen,
sentences us for life to a bridgeless
island of cinders. The street steals
its posters displaying armchairs
and deserts us, leaving us
without a way to anywhere;
but the cinders point to the sea
and the coming of pink jellyfish.

THE CHILDREN OF DRUMS

The guitars do orthopedic calesthenics
on a cougar and cough sea,
and the children of drums
singing the songs of alcohol
float toward the city of blind pickpockets.
Their eyes are hooded
with the sainthood of street corners,
and they accept their drowning
with joyous thoughts of drunken mattresses
and biographies carved on telephone poles.

THE GREEN BIRD

The green bird,
with the eight golden eyes,
sitting still
in the brown, breaking tree
near the lame river,
never speaks
in the dark day
of the sawmill's
overfed children.

THE CALIX OF HEDONISM

The plants of strange hues and bizarre shapes
were beyond our comprehension. Human hands
without bodies were entwined in their tendrils.
The fingernails were smiling, and the hands had
eyes of silver whose winking told us long stories
of how in antique times they tired of the separation
between the animal and the vegetable. Their transformation,
they told us, was achieved by drinking from the calix
of the water lily. We looked at our hands,
remembered how the textbooks had instructed
that our hands were not capable of pleasures
without a brain cabling instructions to our bodies.
We were afraid of the venture, we might lose
what our fingers could give us. We departed
from the field and found ourselves deserted
by what we thought we owned.

FOR A DEAD POET

I

Everyday I planned
to write the letter.
Everyday tiny wild flowers
died under blind feet.
Everyday I heard out-of-date horses
snort at spoken fences.
Everyday I contemplated the cold glare
on my colleagues' faces.

II

Your hands rowed through rivers of wildflowers.
You were living for the green spots
on dead trees.

Now the misshapened streets
have placed a black umbrella
above your body
to block out the goldfinches
that flew over your fountain pen.

III

Once you said all poets who climb
the trees of the ocean
are along with each other.

Now that you have gone
beyond the drowned into the sand,
your voice still speaks
in the silent leaves
that float over the gulf.

IV

I gathered green from the distant leaves
that came from behind the nailed doors of your room,
as I walked through the forests
planted on paper by your fountain pen.

I watched the tears that old schoolyards
would not allow to fall
and irrigate seeds into trees,
but now that your bones
are under the raked piles of autumn,
the acorn fears the burlap bag.

AFTER MANY DEATHS, REBIRTH

My misdeeds scattered money over my face,
and I was granted the embrace
of forceps forged by newspapers.
I lived in an overcoat of sawdust,
and rode on the backs of fallen leaves.
The scars on my eyes brought
the applause of many sightseers;
but the sun's forgiveness burned
the overcoat off my back.
From the blisters arose a poor house
covered with silkworms.
The silkworms pulled a carriage
containing a girl
who never read the advertisements,
and we entered a chrysalis of silence
and arose among a demolished people.

THE HEDONISM OF CHOCOLATE

The hedonism of chocolate is questioned.
A quibble about brochures (wet fingers
around the throat of night: the cellars
are filled with old movie reels).
There are deserts of infinity beyond
the skyscrapers of antique words,
words of fever, words of finance,
words of fat. The wisteria grows
around the worshippers of a frozen room.
Rusty wiring is oozing from the narcissistic tube
of a polysyllabic trumpet. The world
is dancing. The feet are trampling dust
over the silence of hidden voices.
The white dust on the distant radio
is a stoic, and writes with chalk eyes
across the blackboards of time,
and the writing is erased by other eyes.

THE DEAD CHILDREN ARE CRYING
EVERYWHERE

Insomnia brought run-away doorplates,
the slapped eyes of rabbits,
the ashes of robbed stairways,
the wilted brass bloom of real estate.

The children of last night's streetlamp
were limp in their baskets of forgotten moonshells;
their eyes were turned
by the paralyzed hands of posters
away from rain closets
toward the carlight-clipped
gardens of novocained nerves.

SKYSCRAPERS WITH EDGELESS WINDOWS

Skyscrapers with edgeless windows,
no place to stand for a suicide of flight or fall.
Inside the rooms the suntanned scars hum tunes
about the bound wings of birds, and they walk
blindly past the frozen tears in the deep freeze of flesh.
These skilled swimmers in the sea of eyes
carry the tree's blood to the spring ice box,
already overcrowded with the million murders
that feed the walking man.
Ears smile as metal clangs
on the envious backbones of the timid
who hold dead Easter chickens in their wilting hands.

EXORCISM: I

Mathematicians are bottling midnight
and breaking the bottles
on the bricks that crouch
under the whitewashed machine guns
sticking out from coat lapels.
The handcuffed salesman is asking the sponge
if it remembers the salt water
that drips from the eyelashes of shipbuilders.
Accompanied by a grass band of tin bones
the sidewalks are marching toward the weedland.
Wet with rain stolen from movie reels
a tabulator counts the rust spots
that will be hidden in mulberry trees
where they will bite and spread siestas
through the manger fingers of children.
An egret's flight is written into oblivion
by the ink squeezed from the rusty hinged eyelashes
that give prestige to chanting faces.

EXORCISM: II

The radiant swordsmen from old movie reels carve
their initials across young eyes. The desk men
search for unplundered cities. The confetti-haired
daughters of cold air seal the agonized water
in a silver bag. Blue-tile whales line the walls
of living rooms. Maidens with upraised hands
follow the lifted wax daughter. Cracked are
the leaves that once were the frames of light
in an arched age. The fat king with the rusty sword
stares blankly at the libelous mathematics
spoken by those under twenty-one. The ferns
are wilting under the feet of sawdust. The legless
dancers are ushered into a house of smiles.
The lifeguards of canned milk are hiding
the seven razor blades. Where is the shell's alphabet
whose sentences will conquer the fickleness of
erasure. Where is the way to the blue
unlocked windows of the forest? The plastic logs
in the choked fireplace heat the eyes of those
who talk of courthouses and tire sales. What
is the bulldozer doing behind the white curtains?
Mathematicians are electrically plugged-in, and solve
the equations produced by the nylon bag. At the casino
the night is placed on red by bent fenders covered
with dead fish. On their journeys
to cities of ice, pilgrims walk over cemented seed.

EXORCISM: III

Cushions of insane asylum grass dripping
on fingernails from a sky of ashes.
The sterile boat of the stone god's
handshake floating over a night of rust.
Carbon copies blowing over the
rooftops of asphalt ballet dancers.
The ascetics of commerce curling the birds
and selling them as wigs to motor boats
hiding bald heads in the shadows.
Lips bleeding from the passionate kisses
of handbills advertising adults only movies.

EXORCISM: IV

The slapped man sells
his bruised face to children.
The children find blonde handbills in their skulls,
dance to the music piped in by banknotes.
The red dressed wind crawls out
of the cracked stained glass window,
and enters the eyes of the talking old men.
The children memorize the white hair
illuminated on sheets of black lace
that leaked out of the pierced side of the auto.
Promises of aluminum are winking
in the factory built by clicking glasses.
White flags are sticking through the necks
of workmen who shovel steel tears
over the upturned palms of barking hands.

EXORCISM: V

The red spider has left
the wax lily
to find vegetation.
It is dry
here in a land of memorized umbrellas.
The word-wigged auctioneer is selling
the dead sentences' bones.
The healer is stranded
on the other side of the bridge.
He is wrapped in miles
of confetti and highways.
A thousand soft fingers hold
his lips closed.
Where is the man
walking through a forest
of black snails?
He has been murdered by the
adding-machine salesman with the
incorrect answer.
The salesman now sleeps
on a drunken mattress dancing.

EXORCISM: VI

An overture of breaking stars preluded
the arrival of the barge
with the barking
highway builders.
Acid is tossed on the acorn.
Only those with headlights for eyes
will be given a speedboat of aspirin
to race over the river
of captured magazines.
Where is the believer in the sea gull's
hiding place?
He is walking down the corridors
kissed by lead pipes.
On frozen corners hands touch
the bareback movie reels' warmth.
Tears are tattooed on advertised faces
that eat cake from the skyscraper's side.
Blindfolded carwrecks are playing
in a garden of greying hair.
The long sought map is
damp in the hidden closet
and dances to the white saxophone's music.
Where are the flutes of the enchanted mice
that will lead man
to the dark garden thick with indian pipes
and green gourds?
The mice are in the trap found on
the handles of the trophies
that line the shelves of handcuffed springtimes.
Frozen in an eternal handshake, a committee
fills each room.
The newspapers are playing games with eyes.
Haircloth sweaters walk down the corridors
and brag about monosyllables.
The civic leaders educated by ice roll down
a street of bright ashes.
The grey horses have a hundred lonely children
clinging to their manes.

EXORCISM: VII

They are putting the blind pianist into a bag
of cement because he refuses to play an encore
about the abolition of the cow's skull.
They are stitching the mouths of those who tell
stories about the fear spoken by fallen leaves.
Where is the owner of the keys to the invisible tower
overlooking a river of black cloth?
The thistles of the highway are wrapped
in wet money.
An old man is engaged in a conversation
about a vacation in Alaska.
With a department store arrow he shot
an eskimo igloo, and brought home
a cup of melted ice.
A committee met and tied each other's mouths
with the pictures of roses.
The angel with the headache swears
the sky is lead.
The doorknob on the closet door
is broken.

EXORCISM: VIII

The printed children are sharpening their teeth on grindstones.
The moving van carries their eyes away to graveyards.
The muses' hair is put in a sealed tube.
The planks of old houses are pryed off,
and replaced by bird feathers.
The silent stairway that leads to the blue light
has been eaten by the catalogues
of department stores.
The shadows of airplanes erase the illumination
of the rebellious ants' unprofitable activities.
Red silk lounges are floating toward the sky
to replace unemployed stars.
The lizard under the log has been denied
by the crumbling paper blowing in the wind.

EXORCISM: IX

The fishhooks are dropped
by the frozen mouths' spoken cities.
The wildcat is treed by
barking street corners.
The hooked lip is the sign
of the new dispensation.
Bodies of pulverized bone
sift onto chairs of burnt hair.
The murders of ferns are paraded
on rickshaws through the midnight rice fields
under the shadows of the cut-rate liquor store.
An endless list of names is found
on the sidewalks outside
the festival of bent fenders.
A banker drinks dew from the grass.
A suicide's shirt waves from the
insurance policy's flagpole.
Two dice players are hiding
in the berry bush.
Children are sacrificing a vase
to piped-in bedsheets.
The water asks the black-crowned night heron
to wash the water's white hands.

EXORCISM: X

The scars are sunned on the beaches of icicle eyes.
No music comes in the window unless the floor
is covered with fragments from broken lips.
The young man drives along the street of glass stairways
where at the top baroque ice cathedrals melt
and drop tears on the dryness of the steering wheel.
The lead horses of the wine merry-go-round melt
into cubes. The trumpet players gallop
toward the green dots on the back of a black beetle.
Wrapped in green leaves, a lover of spiders
asks permission to live in a deserted web.

EXORCISM: XI

Unseen
the yellow horses with red eyes
arise out of
the slapped man's hair.
Rumors of fighting roosters are circulated
in the confidential rooms of spurred committees.
A mushroom is strangled in the parlor.
The alphabet
that ties the wings of birds
is etched on the horizon of authority.
Wounds are winking
at the silk legs of scars.
A solitary man has run away
to search for mosses.

EXORCISM: XII

The colored lights sending eyes
to basalt prisons. The multicolored
cover drowning the mouth
that kissed the duck's feathers.
The painted steel erasing
the white circles spun by snails.
The yellow painted curb
beating the bare back of silence.
The traffic light dimming
the radiance of the torn sleeve.

EXORCISM: XIII

A hand reaches from a tomato
and waves goodbye to the arriving machinist.
The blue apartment house on the outside
of the pitcher is pouring doves over the stopwatch.
The extreme whistle is plowing a furrow
through a black bag inside the bird cage.
The old rocks are rolling off the tin roof
of the potato patch on the side of last year's calendar.
The lonely fork is looking for a hand
that is wrapped in brown shoe laces.
A jelly fish is singing a song with one word.
An eminent physician is putting six lit candles
in a satchel that was washed in from the gulf.

EXORCISM: XIV

A fistful of moons is carried by lawyers
to whitewashed hands gripping collapsing balconies.
Boats of plastic algae are wrecking
the rented sides of whales.
The cans are crying for their homes
in the tunnels of mountains.
The bare backs of picture frames are offering
bleached fish bones to a handcuffed cricket.
The bewildered cloud is changing its rain
to the street where everyone is dead.

EXORCISM: XV

The mathematical man adds to the string of murders
hanging around the neck of his daily bread.
Every morning a bird falls from a clothes line
rusty in the follies of annuities.
The alphabets are arranged according to
the geometry of hospitals winking at dust.
The cafés are chewing menus
that offer blood from the side of the highway.

EXORCISM: XVI

Gold watches are wearing black wings
in the waiting room of the dead doctor.
Sales tickets are pasted by insults
on the old arms leaning against rusty signs.
The floor of the insane asylum is being sanded
by the steel eyelashes of insurance salesmen.
The skin is broken out with curls
burned on by the kodachrome slides of beaches.
Amputated arms are scattered over
a wide prairie of spilt money bags.
The saxophones are spreading white mold
over the grasses of the ocean floor.

INWARD MOVEMENTS ON MARCH 13, 1966
WHILE LISTENING TO A TV BROADCAST OF
A LUIGI NONO OPERA

1.

Vague birds escaping
from gourds
into a field of
barbed
wire   fish in the stomach movie reels
         become flesh autobiographies

         Rewrite men gathering in white rooms
         all over Germany

the starched collar and the claws of children

         five percent of population
         buying
         second hand trench knives
         and wiping off the rust

lovers exchanging iron crosses on the surfboards of boredom

2.

Snow falling
on
a forgotten
cabbage leaf
         a caterpillar crawls away to wait in sackcloth
no waiting no standing   no waiting allowed when
the alien grass scrapes the wounded shoulder
no investigation for the closing eye

the dead hand cannot feel the bark

3.

Miners walking   I know their lunch pails

Miners walking toward the hollow
eyes
of stone idols printed in newspapers

      the sacks over their eyes will not allow
      the acceptance of the butterfly

they walk toward me speeding   the movie freight train
                           speeding into
                           the aisles

4.

the movie reel body sliced in half by the silver trains from burnt stations

5.

Water out of
falling rocks

                the bird's joy   when drinking a raindrop
                the joy of the duck on wet grass

the glass of water
given the child
His small hands
around the glass

                    let the snake
                    out of
                    the child's jar

6.

Stretchers carrying
men
toward hospitals of
cloth
        someone spoke words not found in
        the rust of the balcony's iron work
the adolescent breaking a match stick

      somewhere a cave lover is being given
      a printed name

7.

An old can projected
on the dyed hair
of a young
girl
        six college professors gather at the
        blood of a dead dog
        to discuss the employment of a
        female colleague

8.

Endless
telephone wires carrying
messages of overnight

        the beds brag about a good sleep

      the torn hair on the street corner

9.

A frog
has
touched
a chained hand

10.

The child's face is covered with the ghost of a tree

        the boy is
                shaking
        the
        birds out of the
sky

                it was just a joke
                the blow torch against
                the cheek

      carve the first name on a back
      and tell the carnival about your love

11.

Smoke outside the house of overeating

12.

Wallpaper sewed on the knocking
      the vote is in   the motor car was elected

13.

Shadows of empty chairs in infinite rooms

14.

A white
marble
block balanced on an old
man's head

a poet dies
he is catalogued

bring the lunch to the dancers
call

15.

The yawn before the burial trench

16.

The silent finger caught in the wire

17.

Chalk marks
on the walls
of the isolation ward

18.

The calculator on a gas tank asking for the wrist
    Sulphur fumes on an
    extended stage
             the hat tipped before the stitches

19.

The skull has no
eyes
to see the bird
tracks
on the damp
sand
          dust on the face being born in the daylight

20.

Adrift among the sleepless signs
Picking the trees out of the eyes of strangers
The secret notebook was stolen by the sparkling colors
Inside the pocket a scrap of cloth ripped from a palm
The sharpened pencils write across a wall
Every city has identical street corners

21.

We look to the factory for the
return of rain

DEAD CITIES

dedicated to Fred Wolven & Rich Mangelsdorff

I. NEW ORLEANS

coffee at unpainted board counter
an old man sawed the wood
he looked in a mirror
not to see the fainting man falling on a cotton stalk
i heard you speaking in the saucer's leaves
a river pressed between the pages of a horizon
legends blew white railing whistles
you dissolved into the laws passed
by the crumbling monastery near a thorn tree
a steamboat with colored lights brought a homicidal piano
I held a black apple in my hand
a cough on a cold corner near a schoolyard
put the fruit back on a tree
a sea of children flowed over the tops of trees
tied together the red feet of the dove
the ark tacked adults-only on its tarred hands
my hands buckled common sense around my waist
as the airplane left the airport
and entered a human eye

my eyes were ginned and burlapped into bales
lobster restaurants jetted their empty glasses
over the redcoated river
the hyacinths had the eyes of strange missionaries
i heard your voice coming from a broken idol
on a neglected road in central america
my hands were eucalyptus leaves

i wondered why i was in the curled iron courtyard
orphans tried to borrow bones
isolde swallowed iodine
worn steps led somewhere to an echo
doors carved with many initials
i heard the loudspeaker
but i could not walk on all fours

a ymca coat tried to borrow money
i thought about the variations on a cat's face
perils sent out tendrils to twist around newspaper words
the greyblue stage theatre did not solve the missing footprint
i remember a medical movie about a man
who could not control his legs
old men going blind and tapping roses

red letters warned of syphillis
i heard snails crawling under distant boards of condemned houses
a girl in a sailor hat stood by a locker in a bus station
the moon had been pushed off a balcony
a blind dove played a piano
across the snow walked a refugee

II. HOUSTON

a bearded man walked down the main street
he carried a sign i did not read
i signed his petition
a stranger scolded me for signing something unread
i replied that i signed the wrong name
that evening someone stole my radio
and i had to do my own singing

III. SAN ANTONIO

wind was cold
i wore a second hand army overcoat
even those present telegrammed their eyes

i asked directions to the opera
was it your voice that came from the blue flower

we spoke vaguely about zoo animals without cages
peacocks brought our dim hands slightly together
antlers came out of a rag
foottracks appeared on snow covering my arms
i held a small stone in my hand
a stigma of a ferris wheel appeared on my forehead

she was gone
a salesman filled a milk machine
a profile seen through a silent space in an arp
from around a bend in a mountain road a desperate banjo
manon touched des grieux
swords and shields collected by millionaires
when the promised land was reached
everyone removed their animal masks

manon wore a sailor hat
smashed diamonds and smashed pears scattered
the electric bulbs in the bus station's
converted whale-oil lamps were being unscrewed
by a dingy hand and dropped on the floor

a hand waved goodbye from a taxi's mink window
her fingers were willow leaves
a carnival barker grabbed my shoulder
explained how to win a plaster angel

IV: DALLAS

at a restaurant counter a stranger talked
asked if I ever attended a harnass race
i lied and said yes
he explained how he outwitted the system

he told me about a boat trip to mexico
he drank nothing but tequila
he said the water was polluted
three men thought they were going to cheat him at poker
but he fleeced them
he asked me if i played poker
i lied and said yes

i wondered why rodin did not pay any attention
to the flower offered by his son

i thought about pierre boulez eating a salad in baden baden
he distained family life

a long stretch of sand with only bird shadows

a long cafeteria line
much talk about the carlsbad caverns
all the males are going to medical school
except one he is going to the argentine
he read appollinaire in french class
its *esperent gagner de l'argentine*
i wondered if i would spend my life
listening to people talk

three days later when i was leaving
i remet the stranger
he looked very depressed
told me he had never seen a harness race
never been to mexico
never drunk tequila
never played poker
he saw all these things in a movie

V: MEMPHIS

a guitar knocked on the walls
nineteenth-century carriages and smiling footmen
snow and hotel blankets not enough
secondhand army coat over bed
diver entered warm waters speared butterfly fish
you were concealed behind a curtain of blood
parking meters clicking in the closet
the once-raped girl in the house with the turret
circles around the tables with the blackforest clock
she is forever playing a violin on the streets of le havre
and watching grey hair fall from trees
musty mattress recorded in account books
strange sounds in bamboo
a green river splashed inside celery

VI: YOU

poison-dripping trees of key west send out immense light.

BETRAYAL

I knew I was different from
those children who were happy
when they overflowed the toilet
in the schoolroom basement,
or when a bruise arose on another's arm.
I wanted instructions on how
to find the way inside a pear,
but my teachers were too busy
remembering the nightclub entertainer's
ten thousand memorized songs.

FROM VOICE TO VOICE

From voice to voice, the cemetery
covered with confetti
carried in a bag of self-love
a sunken cinder
as ash born without a fire

I have listened in a cafeteria
by an ashtray
by a tablecloth
before a finger pointing to the graph

I came expecting to find green fish
swimming in leaves
I came expecting to find at least the lament
at five o'clock
the sadness about helpless hands in traffic jams
the despair about stray dogs

But the fingers smeared by typewriter ribbons
made drawings
honoring the man who can cause someone
to scream in agony

I go from voice to voice

I HEAR SKIN TEARING

I hear skin tearing
and men
with dead owls for eyes
crawling out
towards the vineyards.
They are demented,
and the purposes of their lives
are reversed, for now
they squeeze birds
out from inside shotguns,
and spend the night
crying about what
they did not kill.
They want to play a game
and guess which face
is under the cup
but the wild merry-go-rounds
have disconnected
the telephone from
the hats that hang
outside the white door.
The birds are flying
to remove the flags
that were tied around trees
by hands inside
other pockets.
A fisherman is putting
bandaids on a stone's mouth
for the stone is speaking
about crowds of spotlighted
bodies crawling over
the red table with the eye.
The stone is handing the birds
oranges and the birds
are placing them back
on the trees that refuse

to stand in rows
and wait for the banker.
The jukebox repair man
is screaming from the seat
of a curly haired bicycle
that is galloping
over the water toward
the red boat that is
systematically drowning its sails.
The upside down bodies
in puddles and streams
have waited long for this moment
for now they can rub
the mud from their eyes
and watch the trees
until they give nests
to the birds.

CHASED AWAY

The tree's words that blew in
from the bobcat's twilight eyes
were chased away
by the perverted dogs
trained by magazines in barbershops
Only spiked eyes
protruding out of curbstones speak

On such an afternoon
it is evolutionary to close the shutters
and place over the window
a picture of globed streetlights
and iron balconies
To pretend the guitarist
loves his song
more than the innuendo in the alley
more than the cargo boat
more than the smile
that empties the pockets of the meek

BETWEEN WARS AND AUTOMOBILE ACCIDENTS

Between wars and automobile accidents
this one greeting

Something was said

No language no stone tablet
to carry down the hill of bone
no crowds waiting by the rivers
hidden within blood vessels
Everyone is asleep in the lowland
Only the shadows of crows cross the hillside

They wait by the stone window
by the small oak on the side of the shell road
by the bench in front of the drugstore
No one comes with a language
The words
are in the grave
and one must enter
into the spirit of the dead
to speak
and to be understood
for what is called understanding
is death

Everyone is speaking but nothing is spoken
Everyone understands but nothing is understood
in this separation

A separation during the marbles the curbstone
the twisting chair
Between our notes and our notebook
Between the yellow hibiscus and the yellow hibiscus

In this separation

This apartness of the sparrow
and the sparrow
The bewilderment of seed
The apartness of hours dropped on the electric stove

There could have been
There was
There always will be
a substitute
The remarks about
migratory farmers driving
the cars
that rust in junkheaps
We know our voices are cold
and are often packed in boxes

A carnation placed in the middle
of a foodless table

We carted the donation
to the mailbox
but neither of us
if there were two of us
or even three or four of us
were present
All watched but only one
saw the victory and defeat parade
through the squalid barbershop

In this separation
we become the sea
a sea that cannot clasp
its water
The windows are wet
in the house on stilts
at the tourist resort

Water leaks
through the floor
and sinks
into the unseen land

Glazing over the skulls scattered
through the savannas inside the body
near a broken tooth
near a white path of lime
We hear a hint
even in this separation
a hint spoken by a voice
a high pitched voice
like the voice of a twinspot
there might be a language
with words as real as the yellow orange
on the wilting leaf
from the tibouchina tree

On a separate shore
stevedores carrying
buildings on their backs
but the spider
escapes
He cannot return to Honduras
but there is the edge
of a dead lake
Between two brown seeds
he weaves a language

the silver light along the web
        the moment of the nimbus
        the dark one
        becoming a blaze

BABY SHARKS

Baby sharks in brown mangrove water
carry in the music of their fins
the rumor of your rebirth
My eyes' fingers reach toward
the secret tears in their helpless teeth
and feel the beginning of your hand

THE FURNACE FOR THE STEEL BOYS AND GIRLS

steel boys and girls
wait
for the molds of factory love,
await the furnace
to melt them into one.

only a cartel, a monopoly,
only diamond mines beating
        the backs of africa,
only coffee strapped across
        a peasant's eye.
only macaws with stock market
        tips could supply the cash,
the cash to build the furnace,
the furnace for the steel boys and girls.

LIGHTBULBS'
LENGTHENED EYELASHES
AND STORKS' NESTS

dedicated to the joyous hours
spent in conversation
with Hugh Fox

WHO PLUCKS THE HARP

who plucks the harp
but does not hear in stubble the corn's cry
will be forever
without Eurydice

graves mind born will forever hide
executed oceans and executed trees

eyes
iron wrecking balls
that crack and crumble
perception to gasoline

even insanity has external content

beatings in basements
expulsions from lilies
denials of birth by affadavits from righteous river house

caw a dark caw
in corn's cry

Baudelaire wills
Les fleur du mal
from night sounds
of hungry cats
from cat in Manet
cat by a pillow
hungry cats creeping
from hungry cans
behind restaurants of regrets

where heavy purse
gives form to matter
under silk dress

lonely perplexed
inward angels and animals
fresh from obedience school
bite anima into bits

THE WAY TO THE WAY WANTED

ner durch den zauber
bleibt das leben wach
—Stephan George

way to
way wanted
when stabbed rent
found in movie shower
when worn key
put in twisted keyhole
when prophecy fulfilled
sand dune colored sofa
lavender roses with recessive genes

ropes crowds signs peanut sellers
crowds standing on apple boxes
hands holding accordions
police blowing whistles
waiting for your triumphant parade
pausing as bodiless hoofs tape metal bridges

blocked way
latched leaves
want sleep
sleep deeper than
petite perception
of the stone
bone's sleep
bones resting
on decayed silk
beneath quickly signed
sympathy cards
of cash registers
pushed by bronze fingers

hope as thermostate
on dead body
feels temperature
of temperate zone
hula girls bring
coconut milk

flesh reappears
sees low-priced cotton
under mourning

bodiless arm
gestures toward
slot machines
in exotic ports

blocked way

blockade fermented
in greedy vats
greed grows on
barren soils
where parched hair
watched large carriages
carrying away
magazine pictures
once hidden
under carbon copies
greed plucked
by best mind
who heard tiny crack
in distant cathedral bell

greed becoming tawny
after aging
in caskets
of café life
drawn by Grosz
being poured
into glasses
as ultimate achievement
five bucks
to head waiter
better ten

a riveder la stelle

better twenty
for place
by Queen
in volume
of wounded trees
entitled White Rose

i saw the river

life drilled
by corporals
whose authority
was girl's hand
chopped off at wrist
leaning on
their orthopedic shoulders
as their cars
caught the fingers
of barnfires
and smashed flames
to bits

wanted sleep grave's easy attitude
nights keeping fountain pen factory accounts

waiting for executive's handshake
dictaphone's control of the body swish

i saw river

mussel shell purple riverbanked
my eyes purple

my eyes seeing the overlooked things of the world
crushed cup purple
cracking can rust
insect eaten board

saw river

enter oak roots
walking from bank
under water
becoming covered
with mosses
being touched
by sap
inside white roots
dropped by
water grasses
shadowed by
ibis morning flight
heron night journey

moving toward
moving away from
moving in and out of
ancient alligator subaqueous movements

YOUR VOICE LIKE FLOUR ON FLOOR

Your voice
like flour
on floor
of unloaded
freight cars
spreads over
my hand

whitens a thumbprint

on black pamphlets
received from field
with uprooted tree
two gas tanks
to be buried
in human breath

coral reef
clasps my table
hands with sand lips
kisses from mouse's eye
new stone light spreads
over madeira ambered glasses

but your voice vanished
when we came
to the festival of saddled ponies
somersault of neon midriff

but when the silkworm's whisper
was heard above the silk's chatter
above loud voice of rootless stock report
a hint of your handprint appeared white
on car ruts' black water
but you vanished into perforations
on the poor's ears

rumors spread by green mold
on sawdust pile
said you were
inside buried rain houses
and had a garden of bears

the sky a boulevard of stalled cars

out from gothic church
made of reeds and cattails
on mud's edge
came clapper rail
bringing your voice

six white cats
leaping
in front of
white wall
until wall
is star
and you

ILLICIT BOATS ON OIL DERRICK BEACHES

illicit boats on
oil derrick beaches
celebration by can
shaking silver

men creep through furrows
toward punchcard warehouses
stacked with boxed sanctuaries
sign bills of lading

scribes copy ferris wheel safety bars
protecting distant serfs
whose ears are laden with sweet sounds
coming from under burlap
whose fingers exult
touching loudspeaker's voice

out of whispers about winged couches
tendrils from secret leaders
made of pavement and plate glass
are revived
bound fingers seek
capsules filled with lithographs
and light bulbs' lengthened eyelashes

you

Eurydice you were
murdered by decisions

You came at night
to rooftops
to touch stork's nest
you starved
due to absence of houses

fern finger waves
i think it your finger
although person behind
says it is string
from a surveyor

you

came out of childhood's leg irons
deep under
farewells' foottracks

each summer your breath
moved prickly pear's yellow flower

you were going for an evening walk
in and out of a lost coat's pockets

i reached for your hand
thought i felt the loose hook of a finger
over my finger

we walked toward a country beyond the signboards

CANNOT LAMENT THE CONCRETE

cannot lament concrete
cracked concrete
gathered under backmotor car hoods
carried to mass demonstrations
tossed at opposition's eyeglasses

sand grains' love lost in mixer
lost when invoice was initialed by the blind hand

hand rebelling against attention to yellow parakeet

hand spoken by advertising men carrying shotguns under bucket seats

in space where concrete goose stepped in temporary control of earth
ancient seed prepares dandelions

midway's tormented mouse beheaded woman thirty thousand
        jack-the-rippers
deep wrinkled face present in pocket book as promised by
francis bacon dying with dead chicken in snow

fluorescent light flickering a face
tape brings synthetic drumtap

pollen's enigmas slaughtered by oblivion in taxi cabs

room with unbuttoned logarithms

out of subways prosperina with new man placards
stock exchange revolution
rebellious monks making chalk marks
she walks in mexican sun
does not see cacti
does not see wren's hole in cacti
cannot see darkness standing and falling in wren's hole
cannot see early stone wheel being turned by darkness

she carries messages about knife rips in bus seats
inspires lithographed comrades from wax museum brochures
to tear apart spider webs' community in old men's beards

unwanted stone wheel turns
moves through solid wall without disturbing its posters

spiderweb smashers chase rapt children
from white pool with white fish

she takes guitar constructed from blood vessels
where dreams of cash are hidden
with numb fingertips with hate fingers
she plays songs about love and new man

Ma vlast

palmetto lovers walking down rottening wood and orchid pathways
bending damping knees not to break spiderwebs

his rooster pecks corn from sack hole
cabbage leaves boil on wood stove
he never understood politics
clubbed and left with knife stabs

his banana trees have new supervision
sold to provide rococo nudes for new rich copied from old

on yellow cord strewn shores fishhooks and lost shoes
eyes move toward their ancestors the leaves

sick man in boat
fear erupting
group of masks
sailor fears sea

dancing of fear

submarine garden

seagreen entered
entering seagreen's bones
browned eyes bones from drowned slave's hand

from poet's hand
poet jumping from boat and sinking beneath gull shadows
sinking through clown's face newscaster's face
through tombstones that identify clock

walking under shells
walking under indian burial ground
new buffalo grazing
new carolina parakeet singing
new passenger pigeon cooing
ivorybill woodpecker calling

MANY MOMENTS MANY SPECKS

many moments many specks
yellow leaves brown spots
shrimp leg orange rings
lizard eye

desert brought cow skull
stillborn sands
liturgical salves abortive eyelashes sold
by bent straws on drugstore counters

eye created little bodies little hands
ringed fingered little hands waving from red river before drowning
into blood salt flow in river small salt into sea immense salt

into silence in silence from silence to speech

EURYDICE FERN GIRL WHOSE UNSEEN VOICE

eurydice fern girl whose unseen voice
old copper green adumbrated
blue faience egyptian tomb hippopotamus hinted

waiting eurydice waiting for embodiment
dead girl standing at bus stop
standing by engines completing appointments on parkways

eurydice lingering in ragas played in rice restaurants
your face buried beneath dice tables building theatres around altars
on tropical islands birds of paradise lay their eggs
in discontent of your absence stamped on hands
walking toward suicide under casino garden lemon trees

bored slot machine players bring spear guns
to entertain morning sun with dead angel fish

and with your death in the dying fish color
eurydice's flesh torn and unraveled to float in fragments
toward inward oceans
walking over mud flats far away from new play's applauded lines
away from legislative obtuse faces touching hallucinatory knees
walking touching damp afternoon blue gold oboe sand

bare feet feeling wave left wrinkles
sand pages moon's quaderno

pulling from side speargun laughter

spanish saint sebastian's blood substituting for bull's blood
no tickets required
no turnstile watched by friendly pimp
only scratched knees ripped pants worn stones

guarded balcony dark lace
goya face on eternal orders given maid
as she walks from kitchen to backporch

eurydice barbs rusting nails falling
post sinking into earth blackness

grasses covering
white mushroom umbrellas for katydids
grass blade brown egg symmetry
thin legged green eyes walking
bringing together your face's fragments

ABOVE OR BEHIND BELOW OR IN FRONT OF

above or behind below or in front of
factory window blue paint
opaqueness for hand tacking cedar cigar boxes
bronze nails into brown wood

panther or tiger or cougar or puma or cheetah
something known only to shadows and not to objects
a thing an aura creeping through nerves' jungle
between narrow walls of strange electrical plants
that mail out bills every minute
and demand payment in pain scribbled across leg or arm

harnessing damming turning shadows' wild eyes into seer
seer of pampered overstuffed leather office chairs
that send out weekly allowances
for rock and canned urine armed children

sacred trees grown by sacrifice
grown without game given with gasoline purchase
sacred branches grown for creeping feet
feet becoming sacred creeping
feet wrapped in sacred vines' tendrils

gripped shoulder sacrificed
corridor call sacrificed

ice water pitcher casual lifting lost

every gesture becoming terror
every sparrow becoming sorrow

every wild thing a sacred forest

ORPHEUS AMONG LEMON TREES

orpheus among lemon trees building city of leaves
in spite of guards
building with whispered words sentence to seed
in spite of guards
element night night legacy
night's ancestors gathered fallen leaves into baskets
ancestors who summer walked accompanied by carstruck dog screams
in spite of guards

IF THOU GOEST ABOUT TO COMPREHEND IT

If though goest about to comprehend it, then it will fly away from thee; but if thou dost surrender thyself wholly up to it, then it will abide with thee, and become the Life of thy Life, and be natural to thee.

— Jacob Boehme

contemplation pause lingering on white page
as mind turns white over and over
hears kidnappers rolling up sleeves in upstairs rooms

floor littered overcoated citizens newspaper cut-outs
admiring eyes crayon-drawn on newsprint faces

not respect or envy when winter shiver spoke unraveled elbow
of coat paying its debts

white space loss

scorpion moves over windmill truck's black boards
that once carried skeins of milk
magazine legs hang over sailboat
sending up water drops
bank vaults forever lost

rejoicing as scorpion reverses space

EACH DITCH EACH PERVERSE RAINBOW

each ditch each perverse rainbow
slow seepage carrying unclean pockets

crossing dragonfly shadow lost

ribcage fed tigers touch braille signifying love
feel embarrassment sadness hanging rope arising
hindu flutist basket swungout
snake to devour not decorate

noche oscura del alma

aspirin morning pill night infection spread
television shattered tube

becoming beggar asking for grammar
becoming beggar asking for syllogisms
becoming beggar asking for mathematics

memory gathered deep blood standing
switch can be pulled switch is broken
night will not go out cannot be turned off
not night of darkness but night breaking open attic packages

go where gallows hung innocent man
bury hands beneath gallow's dirt
touch hanged man's thoughts' journey travelling toward earthcenter

accept cruel moments between communion with bo tree and cross

CHILD'S EYES

child's eyes vanished streetcar bar gazes
track torn bricks

melpomene mellifluous dissonant altars
bird songs ranchhouse nightlight burned
bottled finger carved dreams
knee shoved back slapped face
lizard eye fire flies
river large leafed plant

nile river girl strokes blue eyed cat
signboard pulled away cermony sent
nickel dime ceremony wasp parchment printed cosmetic jars
cosmetic jars pulverized butterfly wing filled

clogged closed flesh tunnels
riverbank cut dice stumps
decorator walled steamboats

city eyeball sewer pipe detour

water floating razor blades promise moon closet enticement
rib myth demands sad eyes before hummingbird's guatamala failure

hummingbird take me inside feathers adapt heat cold
adapt dryness humidity
teach me not to be frightened by houses orchards hardens

create within me
tropical rainforests long mossy limbed orchids
mexican californian desert cacti flowers

make my body epheus speech
teach my fern touching fingers to know new sun
teach me
every creature is driven to a pasture with a blow
rites accepted by mankind in the mysteries are
an unholy performance

rib myth water floating tent giving plank giving stone giving
sanctioning quail hunter sanctioning line waiting
millionaire hand waving dreaming poor

cheap brass ring stained finger laughs
unanswerable questions asked in farmyard cemetery sleep
close stadium's sexual winks

i starved hunted fox georgia woods turpentine anxiety
i magnolia bay florida forest treed wild cat fear
i always hunting dog bark followed

cannot dentist holiday hands real estate men
prepressed trigger passed whiskey my mind tame

INVOCATION BURIED

invocation fallen plaster bottom buried
minds swamp filling
invocation skeleton constructing belief application blanks salesman

invocation need flower shaped lizard foottracks across newspapers

must walk must touch invisible sands muse walked sands

unsmeared white temple muse time
wild charioteer unmarked muse arms

grecian adolescents hearing protagoras
two contradictory arguments about everything
swung hair heeded tossed arms heeded vibrated shoulder heeded
riddance ceremony zeus *meilchios* exorcism

zeus *meilchios* never goes only hides
changes objects changes eyes changes eyeobjects

suppliants break beautifully shaped jugs to find cheap wine

must walk must touch invisible sands where muses walked
before *aspasia anaxagoras protagoras diagoras melos socrates* arraignment

before rome man before his kissed hand puts gland above human
beast above angel
puts biology harness on love
in this time invocation need muse need

RAINBOWS UNDER BOARDS

I WAS NEVER TOLD ABOUT

I was never told about
the other side of the
leaf
in the pile

My grammar school teacher told me
many things

She never mentioned the other side of the leaf
Never
the dampness
the tiny drops of moisture
the white
mold
that resembled
un-
sell-
able
cotton

A MORNING

in memory of Ray Newton

dead body stands by sink
after the investigation a few commentaries
spoken in noisy hallways

someone is angry at a slow driver

rain is falling into rowboats
a fish eats the new green of underwater weeds
a sparrow enjoys drinking a raindrop

an eye carries a heavy suitcase over the continents
growing on a sea grape

a sealed jar insists a star is more beautiful than an ant
i crawl along a leaf and find that a yellow aphid has black eyes
i meet a tiny skeleton that i do not understand

an airplane is carrying a corpse who grips two ticket stubs
someone with a loud voice will insult a contented hand

a piece of chalk is writing we cannot return to mathematics
although the drivers over new highways demand exemption from mystery

the loafers and the ambitious have similar fingernails

snails crawl in accord with the green writing of ferns
slugs are finding rainbows under wet boards
the black widow spider is putting wisdom into the trash
a newly emerged moth is memorizing the runic figures on dog fennel

if the paper bag is resisted a brown frog can be seen
through the transparent spots on the moth's wings

i think of Redon and the mystery of the shell
seahorses understand the black lips of the sea
the eye of the jellyfish sees blood on seaweed

the cry on the bridge is unheard in the living room of black vases

i know the mollusca know i have talked with mosses
the words were red and green spiders
each spider had his own alphabet

i await Blake's Prolific and Devourer

the bus is late and those in line prepare to knife the night
cut ears are bleeding in department store show windows

the ant does not bite his brother when a crumb is dropped
i think again of Redon

GRAND CANYON

for Steve Barfield, Silvia Scheibli, Alan Britt and Gerard Robinson

sand winding downward, blurs of brown, red rocks,
fern fossils, shadows of the skin of strange hands,
muddy water, rumpled blankets of sleepless nights,
broken water, white-haired water, water with empty eyes,
water cloaked in holy robes, water in sanctioned cups
held by rock fingers, yellow-sheeted meditative water,
fish fossils, hallucinated hallways of cement lilies
plucking the harp strings of black grass, turquoise eyed
water winking a cloud, wet stairway toward caves of blind fish,
seers counting the tears in backrooms, prophecies recorded
on the white lace of weeds, pale roots whispering
messages through rocks into the eyes of sand, lead water,
broken logs, inlets of reason, fury of reason,
silent temples on the outskirts of rice fields blooming
with cosmic blood, an arch of butterflies,
yellow centers of star flowers,
the sound of shackled horses,
desk minds gazing at loose cloth,
the invasion of red shirts and khaki shorts,
the brochure of nibblers' knives and forks,
necklaces of buffalo eyes with price tags attached,
blindfolded packhorses carrying post cards,
children with drugged wine glasses,
old men selling red-hot irons of paper desires,
surf boards of sleeping pills in deep pockets,
copper into pennies,
nickel into dimes,
trees into banknotes.

A LANDSCAPE OF THE PHILOSOPHICALLY PERPLEXED AND EMPIRICALLY ABUSED, WHO ADMIRED THE POINTS OF GOTHIC ARCHES IN THEIR YOUTH

for Harvey Tucker, Sam Cornish, Hugh Fox, and James Sorcic

the world is not spherical, but is
                        a squeezed
            space
afraid   in a vertical frame.
                        I do not
care what the textbooks and their blackboard
propped-up admirers   say.
Let the learned astronomers talk about
seasons, ellipses, eclipses, stonehenges, and
collect taxes (Now is the time to quote
Meister Eckhart: "If I were a king, and were
not aware of the fact, I should not be king.")
            if you do not believe
the vertical theory, look inside my skull,
            and if you have the capacity to transcend
what is misnamed a *fact*,
                        look inside my skull
and you will see action painters being moved
by their own paint.
            Black paint is holding man
            by the hair and slinging
            his blood across
            the cave of the sky, preparing
            for the hunt that will bring
            man home from the institutions
that have stolen his life.
                        (substitute in the last
line: *his wife* for *his life*)
Tomorrow the sun will start with you, and laugh
at your egotism. The sun will oversleep on a park bench
outside the highest tone of Mercury, which is seven
octaves and a major sixth above the lowest tone of Saturn.
                        We know next to nothing
                        about the life of
                        Claudius Ptolemaeus of Alexandria,
but i believe he lived in
a squeezed space afraid
of its vertical frame,
and created a myth of spheres
because he was too old to have read Kepler.

AN EXAMINATION OF A PAST MOMENT

Hid in a hospital's corner, spiders
showed me a companion under an amputated piano.
We had much in common.
Both were orphans and had ten parents;
but four were always mute behind closed doors,
leaving only six for and against us.
We compared notes on how our many parents
would bring hot milk to make us
have visions of being slot machines
with a surplus of lemons
printed on our spinning lips.
We started to swear to never return home,
but when our oaths were to be written in blood,
we found our veins empty.
We walked in their passageways,
and found the walls whitewashed with milk.
I lost my companion when the piano grew legs
and started to play from a mechanical roll.
My parents multiplied into a million.

PROLOGUE TO AN INTERIOR EXCURSION
NEVER TAKEN

Walked into the cellar of myself;
although cautious, stumbled over a sleeping cactus,
whose thorns tried to keep me upstairs.
Then I remembered my aunt, who wore
white steeples on clock days,
had planted the cactus in the pockets of angels,
who flew softly through the canals of my ears.
My ice cream and jelly bean eyes had put
permanent gold teeth into the cactus' always decaying mouth.
The gold teeth bit my ankle, mocking
my rule in a cake kingdom whose army was overaged.
The teeth were swallowed by rebellion,
but kept biting the roots of interior trees.
I often looked with longing toward
the axes in the hands of box offices;
but by thinking of a wren, I found a hospital.
I would not stand in the corner and study the spiders
when my blindfolded aunt brought a wax island of sirens.
I allowed my wounds to be gift-wrapped
in telephone wires and newspapers.
I saw the stuffed smiles of sofas,
and started downward, but my hands held only feathers.
Found myself on the top step of a shop
where angels of sawdust were purchasing the termites' discarded wings.

TWO RITUALS TO ACCOMPANY SOME SORT OF BIRTHS

Siren's Song: The Way to the Outward

Come downstairs and leave the spiders
whose songs weave solitude in the corners,
swim though a river of echoes,
memorize the testimony of money,
toss stones with the children of silver.
Come to the parlor of painted corpses,
and dine on the pale girl's forlornness.
Come away from the corners and bandage
your bleeding eyes with the bandaids of blindness,
and dance among a masquerade of masked voices.

The Spider's Song: The Way to the Hidden

Find the secrets of *nearby* shadows,
lost in the light of stars.
Go beyond the bright rim
of the fruit bowl in the parlor's hands,
fall into webby darkness
underneath the avenues of smiles.
Descend through holes
chewed out by prairie dogs,
find the cave fish with no eyes,
and see with his wisdom
the way through the wounds
of the voices with masked words.

AN OLD MAN WALKS DOWN STREETS
OF WATER

An old man walks down streets of water,
streets whose signs are backward,
where the house numbers have lost their confidence,
where the ones, the threes, and the sevens
are perplexed in their loneliness.
Finds himself shouted at by office boys
happy with their bow ties and Christmas trees.
There is no drowning in this bottomless water,
for past mistakes push the nose above the surface.
There are flashes of terror in the water.
The fish nibble at the blindfold woven from grey hair
and let in fragments of fragments: bones and eyelashes,
the burnt hair of the overpaid Venus,
the white dust from the tower of love.

A SUDDEN COLD IN FLORIDA

On this morning of sudden cold in Florida
I think of a slave
suffering among jade vases in ancient China.
I see a bent man
bringing her a scroll
inked with a faraway blue mountain
seen through the leafless branches of a fallen tree.
I see her turn away
toward the sunflash
on a galloping silver saddle.

MANGROVE ISLAND

At first only the eyes present
orange and yellow weeds
reflected over brown water
dark water
dark as a nun finch feather
or burmese cat's fur

Restless eyes
seeing increases desire
to sprout roots
to grow beneath the emptied shells
deep into the brown earth
to speak with the whiteness of roots
to hear the language
from someone who has faced buried things

Eyes turn upward
away from the red
canvas caught on a mangrove
upward toward the sky
upward to the buzzard
but still no turning
away from the always
present desire to sprout roots
The buzzard does not write
poems
although his destiny makes him
a poet
He does not write poems
because he is not conscious
of how he lives
The cow's eyes
are hidden from us
by the soft music piped
into the steak house

The white aproned butcher
clips the eye's roots
protecting us from the mangrove's growth
an island gathering all things
the bloated frog
the floating dog
the broken raccoon
the hand that never touched the cord
to start the speedboat

Halophytes the Greeks called
the mangroves
Salt on the leaves
fisherman salt their soup
by boiling the leaves
My eyes feel the thickness
of each leaf
a slick leathery surface
that will never
be shoes
Each leaf has its own
ocean
Each leathery leaf
a leather-winged bird
with buds of feathers

Avicennia nitida is a special variety
named for avicenna
avicenna who saved aquinas
from the frozen stones
from the stiff hands
from the musty harbors
to become wrapped in the mummy cloth
of systematic thought
to be buried
because his eyes visited
the barbershops of logicians

Orange growers use mangrove wood
for smudge
to save their summer vacations
for the pulling
of slot machines in Kingsport
Their rootless eyes
spin around and around

Somewhere in a dark place
under shadows
left by those who ran away
under leaf shadows
perhaps in another place
perhaps behind a twist of roots
comes a timid sound
a soft sound
a sound as if filtered through cotton
the song of a painted bunting
a bird so beautiful
it must continually hide
The eye listens
The eyes feel the birth of roots
roots reaching into the water
the beginning of an island

A STRAY HORSE IN ASIA

The stray horse stops
looks downward
hears starshaped flowers
blossoming
out from fuzzy leaves
struggling
through the crevices
in a war of rocks,
listens to the galloping thousands,
sees through the dust
each holding his head high,
not looking up, down, or behind
at the masters with the knotted ropes.

CHINESE POETS

Chinese poets seem always to be in
bamboo exile,
always walking through the mists of marshes,
always passing
an old fisherman with an empty net
vague against a yellow sky,
always thinking about the shadows
of a pear tree across
the painted fingernails of a young girl,
always
hearing unseen birds
deep in the thick reeds, the voices
reminding of squeaky
hinges
on the gates of their
wrecked
homes.

WASTED TIME

I awoke when
I heard
the oleanders breaking.
A car was coming
through my front yard.
It seemed to be going
very slowly
and was heading
for my bedroom.
When my wall
started to collapse,
I resigned myself
to receive the pain
from crushed ribs.
I even quoted Marcus
Aurelius and Epictetus.
Once I thought about
running away
but I remembered Roland
and his unused horn.

SAMSON AT GAZA THE DAY BEFORE THE ATOMIC DESTRUCTION

Now blind
broken by an echo
bouncing off
collars and cuffs
molded in iron.

But now confronted
by a horror
greater than the horror
of never seeing again
the tanager's red flash
through the green pine
greater than the horror
of never seeing again
the variations in the dirt's color
around the mole's hole
the horror of seeing the future child
imitate my past acts.

Children march out of my old eyeballs
and leave their fingers hung
in the dials of broken telephones.

Still a greater horror
the horror of a choice
for I am told
by pencil marks across cartons
in long storerooms
that tomorrow I must destroy
an entire civilization.

Once when a boy
I walked alone by a river
and my cheek was touched by a fern,
and I heard a green river
splashing inside this fern,

and green water drops
suspended in air
made an annunciation
about a new birth
that would happen
when I climbed the walls
and went to the place of gourds
and entered a gourd.

When I returned to the schoolyard
the schoolboys that gathered
around the machine shop
saw the impression of the fern
on my cheek.
They laughed and sneered
as their fathers had taught
them to laugh and snear
when seeing the strange.
I became afraid
when I saw my future self
walking alone on streets
and being shouted at
from passing automobiles.

As we entered the circus ground
a girl broke away from my hand
and she smiled at the carnival poster
of a bright purple man
sticking pins in a girl's legs,
and she left me
to become the mistress
of that painted man.

I saw my future self staring at cracks
in hotel doors
and never knowing love.
I refused to listen

to the voice of the green water drop
rubbed its companionship from my cheek
joined the boys at the machine shop
and the girl left the bed of the painted man
and retook my hand
and we wore the dog collar of electricity
generated by the signboard.

Tomorrow the trumpet signals the festival
and the citizens unwrap themselves into streets.
They shall cheer silver suits whose shoes
will walk on moons and whose claws
will bring back samples of moon dirt.
I must go to their festival and pull
the columns from their centuries.
Now I know only I must
destroy a civilization,
but I cannot remember why.

I have asked the boys
at the machine shop
and the girl who held my hand
and they do not know why,
but they insist
that the civilization
must be destroyed.
I have asked for answers,
but the only sounds I hear
are airplane propellers
moving inside my arms.

ECHO AND NARCISSUS

for Fred Wolven

Echo

I am the rain
whose barefeet touch
the seedpods asleep in your nerves,
who comes to wash away
what was spoken in old men's whispers,
who comes to dissolve
the billboards blocking
the way to the unknown room.
I am the rain, the splash
inside the fern that covers
solitude with a green cloth.

Narcissus

What I see in this pond
is sadness staggering through eyelashes.
What I see in this pond
is the bivouac of terror on the forehead.
But I hear a voice, a voice
that sounds like the voice
that rattled a gourd
on a misty prairie morning
when the corn opened into a leaf.

Echo

I am the rain that falls
with the unique imprecision
of the mystic's conversation
with the flown goldfinch.
I am the rain that unties the eyes
from the memorized street.

Narcissus

Between the sadness and terror
the frog leaps from the water lily leaf.
Now the frog is only a memory,
but the frog might have been another deception
of this mirror that is water,
just as this voice that sounds
like a hummingbird's wings
still and moving over a banana flower
might be another deception
of this mirror that is water.

Echo

I am the rain
that turns the iron gate
into an oak twig
surrounded by sea light.
I am the rain
that sends the lightning flash
through the old house's sagging door
and illuminates the spiderweb's secret.

Narcissus

If I turned to see
the source of this voice
would the voice be only a sound
in empty space?
I once turned toward a voice
that spoke about a talking rock
that was buried deep in clay,
and after I spent my childhood digging,
I found my hand placing a silver dollar
on a number, and there was
only empty space.

Echo

I am the only voice with a body.
I am not the voice coming from the waving hand
printed on the balcony.
I am not the voice in the electric leaf
blossoming out from the false log.
I am not the voice coming from the crimson
painted on kneecaps before cameras.
I am not one of the many voices
said to have bodies
but who have no bodies.
I am the only voice with a body,
turn and touch my body,
my rain body.

Narcissus

I turned before
once toward a voice
that sounded sweetly
as if her shoulders were sleeping wildcats
in a humanless and dogless forest,
but when I turned
I discovered the source was a microphone.
A well digging machine was being oiled
and polished by chained hands,
and then there was nothing but empty space.
Nothing touchable,
only empty space.

Pond

Only empty space.

Narcissus

And then more sounds:
sounds from seaweed dried
and stuffed into chairs,
sounds from the wood chipped off totem poles.

Pond

More sounds.

Narcissus

Sounds from the poisoned sandwich
given the imported worker,
sounds from the tree branch
carved into cabinets for scorecards.

Pond

More sounds.

Narcissus

Sounds from the sunned skin
that had no body—
the skin and the suncolor
only a projection from a kodachrome slide.

Pond

Sounds.

Narcissus

When I turned away
from what was supposed to be present

and turned back toward the pond water,
one eye was blind.
I turned from my only identity
to enhance its existence
with what I was told
would enhance its existence.
I was told
by the involuntary smile
that appears on the respectable citizen's face
when he hears about a successful criminal,
and I believed the smile.
Now I am without belief,
for everything believed
has resulted in the loss of an eye.
Although now I hear parrots splashing
in the rain water caught in a tree hollow,
and I hear the splashed water
falling on a leaf that seems to touch my cheek,
I am afraid to turn.
Afraid.

Echo

Without your touch
my flesh will become
the printed page in a magazine
that a child will hide in a hibiscus.
The wind will tear me out
and send me down sidewalks
and over vacant lots until stopped
by the bent iron of a street sign,
and there I will whiten into blankness.
I can only remain a body
through your touch,
only through your touch.

Narcissus

I am afraid.
I have hoped too many times
and each time
what was hoped for
was not worthy
of being hoped for.
Only one eye left.

Pond

Do not turn, Narcissus, do not turn.

Narcissus

Another voice, but a more familiar voice,
like the voice
I heard when a child
after with rocks I had chased away
a flock of crows who had dropped
their shadows on a blue road.

Pond

Do not turn.

Narcissus

This familiar voice, a voice
that seems to have been speaking for centuries,
that spoke from the axe of my great grandfather,
that spoke from the trophy room of my grandfather,
that spoke from the bulldozer owned by my father,
now speaks from my reflection.

Pond

Echo
is being carried away.
The rain
is being put
in large vats
and sold
by the cupful
to the thirsty.
Large armies
have been drafted
to protect these vats,
to keep the thirsty
from stealing the water,
to make the thirsty
serve the vat owners
before they can drink.
Echo is in the vats.

Narcissus

I cannot understand
this voice.

Pond

Your understanding is gone.
Your understanding
will never again
be the source
of a decision.
All decisions will be made
by the vat owners,
but you will never
see the vat owners,

for they will live faraway
in large houses,
protected by police dogs,
tear gas and armies
paid by a drop of rainwater.

Narcissus

My arms move
but I have not
told my arms to move.
I stand but I have not
told myself to stand.
My legs move
but I have not told
my legs to move.
I step into the water
but I do not
want to step into the water.

Pond

Step Narcissus step.
There is no longer a reflection,
not even a one-eyed reflection.
There is nothing
on the water
to prevent your stepping.
Step down into the water,
into a darkness
that is not water,
into a darkness
that is not darkness.

TOUCHED BY THIS WATER

Touched by this water
Water as inevitable as
the hand of bone
as endless as the burlap bag
around the reaching winter fingers
as brave as the ferns
in the painted lips
of the rotting mask
This water that touched
and will touch
the echo in each minute
that dropped from
the stringy paws of the sea turtle
This water that has flowed
through the sadness
of the centuries
soured the wheat sacks
in dead cities
and arose an angel
with a body of air
that became
a tree with golden leaves

LOGGERHEAD SEA TURTLE

Before the salt seaweed blew
back and forth on a skeleton boat
in a Cartheginian shipyard,
when Aeneas was only a noise
in a conch shell,
when Dido's kisses were being planned
inside a sand grain,
the loggerhead turtle abandoned the land
for the sea,
and now he carries
in his motions my night.

RITUALS

1.

highest part is darkness

every act is
exterior
and lost in the landscape

even the
stars
are our enemies

2.

reconcile yourself
to greyness
before
darkness

a blindfold would lose
image

desire is enemy
to watch

flicker of match
can lose
image

3.

covet image
while hands
are tied

caterpillar
on sidewalk
is not image

caterpillar
on sidewalk
is image

covet caterpillar

4.

image's side
is black with arrows

go to land
of no bleeding
and hear
image

5.

trust not theory

theory is axe
to enter unseen

theory is lost
in cutting

6.

enemies are
waiting

to make known
direction

under the roadsign
image
is lost

SEPARATION BY NEWSPAPER HEADLINES

I am here captured by freedom
while you lap
the barbed wire.
They tied my hands
when I tried to break geography.
Once we always flew together
if the plane crashed
we could die together, but
when I purchased
one ticket
and stuffed the papers
into the portfolio
I could not foresee
our separate sufferings.

CONTEMPLATING THE WESTERN IDEAL OF CONQUEST

On mangrove island
by a dark stream trickling over
redorange fungi
on fallen branches
I saw a vireo
and I said,
"Yellow and grey bird
will I ever
be able to stay
lost in labyrinth
to praise the hoof
to honor the hide
and to tell
how much I love
all animals
and all vegetation
and ultimately
to lose my country
to become fused
with the divinity
of animals and vegetables,
to live in the life
of a mangrove leaf,
or will I remain
forever standing
in rooms or on
concrete holding
unwound and
rewound thread."

BUFFALO, REDWOOD TREES, AND OTHERS

Cannot believe it happened
after all the running and rains,
but the event is limp in my hands.
Someone else will have to do the digging.

Must search the alleys,
looking under garbage platforms for plates,
trying to discover the saucer
to see who slipped out the poison;

then I must learn the bottle,
the drug store, the government.

RAINBOWS WITH WRONG COLORS

Have tried many times to keep
the streets of childhood from returning,
but my small feet burning from sunbeaten sidewalks
keep walking through the night waters.

Strange sizzles emanate under the feet
as past combines with present
sending up rainbows with the wrong colors
and saying there will never be a covenant.

MY BROTHERS' EYES

They called themselves my brothers
Their eyes resembling traffic lights
flashed three colors

Mainly red
when doors appeared on the butterfly's eyes
Mainly yellow
when a girl hid a goldfinch from a shotgun
Mainly green
when a bulldozer came to the sea oats' inwardness

WINDOW SHOPPING

Grabbed by the building's claws
I was
transformed into a brick.

Placed between bricks,
cement spread over my eyes.

I saw dead sand.

FOR SOMEONE WHO HAS KNOWN
THE DESPAIR OF HOPE

What has been brought
to this green island
What gnawed away this island
What sanctioned thing
ate its way through burlap
to bite the source the human voice
to separate the sandgrains
to put the sand asleep in battleships
to awaken sloshing among blood in strange waves

You knew
Your answers came from walking
out of subways on cold nights
holding the hand of the aberrant
suffering the agony of embarassment before the insane dance
Your answers came from your nightly reading
of logic spoken by automobile hoods
but you could not speak the answer

We had heard
the stray bullets of the nightwatchman's nihilism
We had heard
the howls of the starving huskies
We had seen
the blood creeping from the redwood's gashed side
But you were closer
for your body had been invaded
by the secret meetings of overpaid parachutists
You saw the nail
driven through the spinning top

Your face was too earnest
to be covered by the laundered cloth
with the afterdinner joke
You were too devout
to lean on the piano in a stenographer's dream
You still carried the bloodstained love
from antique crosses in the monastery behind your eyeballs

I watched others speaking about you
Taking their blind autobiographies
and rewriting your life
The garden rose the embossed rose
the heavenly rose the earthly rose
became angular and price-tagged
in the narcoticism of the commonsense remark
Others could not speak you

I wish I had known you
before your love without arms
had wrung its own neck
and frightened the willets on the shoreline
I wish I had known you
when you were a child
although being prepared
not yet knowing about those
kissing the trapdoor in the concrete
not yet knowing about the cut fingers
that ripped open the wire
around the hemmorage in the hencoop

I wish I had known you
before headless you wiggled in your own hands
Love is terrible
because it gives sight to the eyes
takes the sheet of words off objects
brings one face to face
with the battered eye of the ancient alligator
with the limp body of the BB filled bird

Because it brings one face to face
with the mind fallen on the turtle's back
as the turtle returns to the gulf to die.

ETERNAL VOYAGE

for Steve Barfield, Silvia Scheibli, Alan Britt, Paul B. Roth, Richard Collier, and Gerard Robinson

The voyage started on a boat
with its painted eyes painted out,
faint blue eyes slightly visible under white splashes,
dim eyes receiving dim messages from wood,
hacked wood, hewed wood that had lost its forest meaning,
wood separated from underground streams
and the blind worms' caresses.

The boat was once named *Argo*,
but its name was painted out,
and no new name given,
for everyone was afraid
to identify its purpose.
No one would speak about
the spaces being cleared
in warehouses for boxes
of something said to be golden.

When the crew boarded the boat
each had the same face and the same body
as the captain.
Each had heard the ghost fungus
talk in its sleep.
Each had been somnambulists
among moons brought by mollusca shells.
Each had joined the seagulls' shadows
under water and pulled wood strips
from sunken lobster traps.

The boat departed from the shore
lined with frightening funereal jars.
The crew had hoped to forever leave
the thoughts about ashes.
When they passed an island
where all wild flowers had been picked,
they listened to electric songs

explaining how praise of the rich fisherman's saliva
would silence the ravishes and rages of minutes.
The crew immediately unwound
their hair from the nests of hummingbirds,
separated themselves forever
from the interior woodlands and banana trees,
developed distinctive features
in order to be easily identified at bank windows,
began speaking a language different from the captain
now rapidly aging and speaking in mumbles.

The crew now perplexed
by the direction of the captain's telescope,
by his eye twitching and hand trembling,
gathered under the nets' shadows
told stories by finger gestures
about a land with an eternal carnival:
snowfrozen beheaded woman, wine-color eyed rats
captured in Paris sewers by unemployed soldiers,
rifles shooting away the river's clothes
and revealing naked diamonds.

From his coat pocket
the captain took
an old yellowed scroll,
read in an indistinct voice
the directions
which he no longer understood.
He read they were to go
to a swamp where dragonflies
unscrewed windows from cattails
and placed them on sand grains.
They were to look through these windows
and see the earth's center
and someone there would hand
them a warmed pebble.

The crew disregarded his orders,
shouting he was too old for wisdom;
he had already carried them
too far in the wrong direction.
They wanted to go to a port
where a supper club had been built
over tern eggs
and cheetah coated girls
brought a burning manger
to each table.

Each day the crew's complaints increased.
They complained that the cargo crates were empty.
Should contain small hoofed animals
to be exchanged for adults-only movies
showing the cloth being lifted
from a left-handed moon.

The crew mutined,
but the captain could not understand
the rebellion,
thought it was a halloween party,
ordered the cook
to bring out a pumpkin,
and then went to the ship window
to ask an inlooking fish
about why the postman
had brought his pension.
When the fish turned away,
the captain asked the fish's tail
why his children had come to visit him
during visiting hours at the rest home.

The crew sat the captain
in front of a television set,
anchored the boat

on a shore littered
with dead iguanas.
They stood knee deep
in salt water and laughed
at the slow creeping
of exhausted foxes.

The place was a lava island
where Empedocles had jumped
into a volcano
after he had written
love created the world.
His hand bones holding
a petrified pencil
glistened
under the crew's flashlights.

THE SUBMERGED FERN
IN THE WAISTLINE
OF SOLITUDE

ON A CLIFF IN MAINE AND EVERYWHERE

1.

The paved fogdimmed road led
upwards
        to the sign,
                fading
squared black letters, giving
hazy information
                about a family,
their cemetery.

                A dump truck,
emptied, disappeared behind
a boulder.

Still separated
                from the sand
I faced the misty ocean,
                a dark cross
flew towards me,
                changed
into a blue swallow,
                and then
an upward movement,
                blazing
cinnamon,
            a dart downward,
disappeared
                somewhere in what
was my foundation.

At the road's edge
                recently poured
gravel,
        whitespotted, bluespeckled,
dustless.

Not yet walked upon,
not yet pressed to smoothness, to
evenness,
            to nondisturbing
indistinction.
            The gravel's sharp points
pressed
            through my shoes.
I glanced
            at the shapes
                        left
in the air
            by the swallow's
absence.

2.

            A white stone wall,
cemented, troweled, whitewashed,
spoken many times
                        until
                        no longer
stone,
            but a disembodied whiteness
curving
            through the fog.

3.

            A touch
of the white wall
                        leaves white
on the hand.
                        Not a sacred marking, not

a smear from the air's ashes,
                            but
insubstantial
            chalk,
                    white hair
from the mathematics
                    scribbled
on a blackboard,
                    mumbles in the
finger's
            folliage,
                    easily rubbed off, easily
silenced,
            but forever permanent,
invisible
            in the loudspeakers
                            of the eye's
migrations.

4.

An opening in the wall,
                    a gap
through the teeth
                of the nets
thrown over
                ancient voices, two
cement steps
                downward
                    and a step
to the side
            of the gravel,
                    orangish
sand.
        In a handful I hear
                            the bone

separated from the fur
                and centuries
of dead wings.

Closer to the breath
                of the buried
swallow.

5.

                On a nearby ledge
breaking through
             bluish rock
a pitch pine,
           her wild hair
galloping
            towards the starfish
behind the
          sky's cloth.
                Her roots
hear
      through the rock
            the swallow
fluttering
       over straw
            in a dark crevice.

6.

Through the twisted branches
                the distant
cliffs' bluegrey tips,
          a passing
thumbprint,
        bluegreen forest beneath.

Farther north,
　　　　　higher cliffs, colder.
There lives the petrel,
　　　　　a bird
that comes inland
　　　　　only at night.
Incubation is long
　　　　　and the petrel
leaves before his poems
　　　　　fly.

　　　　　The poems
are left on the rocks
　　　　　to grow
from what
　　　　　the petrel scooped
from the ocean.

7.

I remember
　　　　　a swallow flying
out of a barn
　　　　　in Minnesota,
a swallow
　　　　　feeding her young
on a rafter
　　　　　in New Hampshire,
a swallow
　　　　　sending a shadow
over a buffalo
　　　　　in the
　　　　　　　　　Bronx
zoo.

8.

          I think
of Baudelaire's albatross,
               the
awkward
      walk across rock.
          Of Rilke's panther
circling
       through a black iron
eternity.

          I remember
myself
      in Tampa's Busch Gardens,
my hands
       touching a white wall
as I watch
       a fat
          black leopard
relaxing
      on the branch
         of a
cement tree.

9.

        A baby
turning on a lathe
        being cut
into a pattern
      by the chisel
of words,
     gestures,
        smiles,
frowns

from the unseen sides
of the dice
tossed down
the long corridor
after the
showing
of the stag movie.

10.

Along the path
the sumac flower's
red fruit,
momentarily
a
reddish purple. Never
the same color. Infinite
variations of reds
and purples.

An evaporating bird of blood
flying through the menaced eyeball.

The sumac
only
a fixed and permanent
color
when a name in the mind.

But the name
a witchdoctor
following a firefly
through a night
of heavy rain.

Only
absolute, everlasting

when a
swallow
inside the human body,
but without
the sumac's
everchanging
colors
the body
disappears,

11.

Below the path
beneath its sand
dark grey rock,
sunstruck pink rock,
brown rock,
redbrown rock.
Limpets,
periwinkles, sea snails
clinging,
listening to
the swoop
of the swallow's
arrival and departure
from the cave.

12.

On the blue rock
tidal pools
pink
bottomed,
pink rock crust algae
bottomed,

                    yellow lichen spotted,
an earth star.

The tidal pool pink
                    similar
to a pink
            in a Sassetta
journey
            towards a star, not a
star in the sky, but a
                    star
on the ground,
                    an earth star
among
            goldfinches.

In Sassetta
            white birds
                        fly over
pink turreted towers
                    as heads, turbaned,
bare, turn
            towards
                    the earth star.

Here in
            Maine
                    blackwinged gulls
fly over
            a deep green ocean,
                            over
bright painted lobster buoys, vanish
in the fog,
            their cries, mews
left in the rocks,
                    in the arm.

Their cries have become
                    granite
and flesh.

          A small brown dog
running in Sassetta
                    runs again
in the brown streaks
                    through
fallen rock.

13.

A buoy
          ringing through the fog,
a vague boat
               guided by a
                         blur
moves
          according to necessity
and a blind
               surrender to necessity
towards
          sunken lobster traps
and the lobster's
               plugged claws.

                    Three
fogblued islands,
               white wave
surrounded,
          arise
               a light brown,
               the same
shade of brown,

                    as the mounds
of dirt
        left
            on farmland
by poisoned
            gophers.

14.

Out of
a blue space
the same blue
as the swallow's wing
when
shadowed
by a rock ledge
come disturbing faces
that
destroy the blue
and the space
and all space:

the goodnatured face of the preacher
breaking the back of an alligator in the everglades

the respected and honored face of an ambassador
killing for entertainment a kudo in Africa

the convivial faces of the towspeople in New Mexico
going out with shotguns to kill the surplus of cowbirds

the proud face on a causeway throwing a spear at a shark

all the same face

a movie fan watching on the screen
a dagger being driven into his wife's
box of costume jewelry
a lawyer mowing the fingers
sprouting in his frontyard briefcase

15.

        A pump
handle creaks
         in the memory.
A cold Georgia morning,
            sounds
from a sapsucker
        pecking on
a pecan tree.

In a Florida orange grove
a shotgun ends a sapsucker's life.
The grower records the coins gained.
Uses the profit to buy a newspaper
with stories about how a woman
ate up her newborn baby, how a
woman gave birth to six dogs, how
a man was raped by six women.
Then he hides the newspapers
and presents his son with a
toy machine gun, a football helmet,
toy replica of a corvette,
and some fishing tackle.

        The night's strong winds
had scattered
         over the clay earth
pecans still in green husks.
         The funeral
at four. The kin uneasy about

the will. Who gets the windmill,
the fishpond, the timber, many
trees were ready to sell for lumber.
The dead man's wife dying in a
featherbed. Cancer. Who will get
the tractor. Who will get
the aging mistress selling shirts.

         The pump
is primed from water
              poured
from a bent coffee can.
          A taste of
iron in the
      water,
           red
clay specks
       in the
         water.
Rust on the fingertips.

A white rooster
        crows
            from
the sagging
       falling
           greyweathered
boards
     of the muddy pig pen.
Rusty nails,
       time eaten,
            partially
fallen
   from
      the fence post.

Screams

from the
     bedroom.
Coffee cups
    paralyzed
       in
the air.
  The cup in the hand
with sunburnt knuckles
       has a
crack
   in the shape
     of a curled
hair.

Out on the carefully
      clipped
frontyard grass
    stands
      a
plaster angel
    won at a
carnival.
    The angel's
glaring white painted enamel skin
draped in
    a blue and green toga.
Bright yellow
    waved
      plaster hair.

The eyes
  have
    faded
      away.
Only a few tiny blue specks
on
  blank eyeballs.

16.

A tree thicket, gum, oak,
chinaberry, unknown trees,
between
        newly plowed peanut fields.
Dislodged
        pale white peanuts
                glittering.

Woods becoming
        narrower
           and
narrower
      each year.
        More
crop land needed.
        More
money needed to buy
      the newly
invented farm machines, to
send
     the children
        to
           private
schools,
    to
      avoid
        a schoolyard
where
     children of different colors
talk.

Bulldozers murdering
        trees
          and all
the animals, birds, insects
        that

live with these trees
　　　　　to bring
more money.
One of the few bears
　　　　　still living
in the Georgia forest
　　　　　murdered
and placed
　　　　　on a doorstep
　　　　　　　　as a
warning.
A victorian house, surrounding
porch,
　　　curlicued,
　　　　　　of an old
lady,
　　　who once gave frontyard
parties
　　　　but who now lived alone
with fourteen
　　　　　cats,
　　　　　　　　six orange,
two grey,
　　　　one white, one black,
and four mixed,
　　　　　burned
　　　　　　　　as a
counter warning.
　　　　　　　　　I,
hoping to find
　　　　　a hummingbird,
recalling
　　　Pablo Neruda's
"Oda al picaflor,"
　　　　　turn
a squeaky bird call.

                        Vine shadows,
large red
            tubular flowers,
                        many
fallen,
        yellow streaked,
                        on
piles,
        moist and
                    fungi stuck
together,
            of brown speckled
yellow spotted
                green gum leaves.
                On a
rainsmoothed clear spot
of blonde earth
                    a turtle.
His shell,
            yellow marks
on black,
            speaking a language
as holy
        as mysterious
                    as
the language
            of a Paul
Klee.
        More mysterious,
                    deeper.
The mingling
            the coalescence
of the
        sun's
            the
                wind's
                    the
rain's
        the grasses'
                voices.

17.

My bare feet feel
                the dampness
under the leaves,
                the earth's
dampness,
              the earth's invisible
star.
I feel
      the
          earth
              moving,
moving with the motion
of the
          brown
divine worms.

18.

                My foot
displaced
        a
            leaf
                the worm
wiggles, twists,
                struggles.
The light is not his
dwelling.
          He lives under
the fallen leaves'
              dark sky.
He shines with his own
light,
an earth star.

19.

Haydn's *Seasons*,
                    the music
comes
        into my mind,
                        a music
when man felt
            wanted
                    on this
earth,
claimed
        God wanted him.

Not the new music,
                    Cage,
Lygetti,
        Berio, Nono,
Stockhausen.
            The new music
music of unwanted man,
                        man
the intruder,
            the destroyer,
the species
            that failed.

The new music not a
lute concerto
                for an
overfed,
        half asleep man
wearing
        silk pants and a
wig,
    pretending
                the earth
is his dominion.

The new music not a
music for, no music for
the current man
                  his mind
pricked and scratched
                  with
needles
        from the hypodermics
of murder,
            the murder of
the earth
            and the creatures
of the earth.

The earth is
the quail finches'
the rattlesnakes'
the sharks'
the grasshoppers'
the bobcats'
the scrub oaks'
the sandspurs'
            dominion.

Man the intruder, the
unwanted.

20.

        How can one
        ever atone
        for being born
        a human being

Wash the oil
from the cormorant's
feathers

Try to convince
a fat rancher
that a coyote
is more important
than the color television
that the
profits from the
copulation of cattle give
Refuse to sell land
to phosphate companies and
not become respectable
with the income
Write to your congressman
asking that he sponsor a bill
appropriating money for research
to prevent the suffocation of fish
telling him you control
a block of ten votes
and will contribute
to his campaign fund.
You also might add
that you would like
to see some research done
on how to protect
sharks from human beings
and how to keep people
from interfering with
the shark's dominion
Promise your congressman
a large donation
Protest the cutting of
trees to make way
for telephone wires
Picket the offices
of those who entitled
themselves land developers
and insist they be honest
by calling themselves
land destroyers

Burn all signs
that use the word progress
as an excuse for destruction
Spread propaganda
that ponds creeks streams
rivers bays gulfs and oceans
are superior to swimming pools
Do not eat
in the restaurant
owned by the man
who hunts in Africa
Boycott the movie nude body
of the actress
who wears coats
made from animal fur
Stop your subscription to a newspaper
that publishes a picture
of a young boy
who shot a leopard
unless properly labeled
human sadist and degenerate

Protect the
purple pink skin
the golden stripe
of the caneback
rattlesnake
crawling
in the peanut field

How can one atone for:
        for filled bays
        for roads that cause the eagle to leave its nest
        for hens imprisoned to lay eggs in cages
for the drowning of surplus baby roosters
for the emasculation of cattle
for the rodeo horse's chained gonads

for the pike in the bull's shoulders
for the ripped open belly of the cock
for alligator wristwatch bands
for caiman wristwatch bands
for dancing elephants
for bicycle riding chimpanzees
for wagon pulling ducks

Man
the
excresence

21.

i seek the reddish fur of the moonlight
when it creeps from its burrow and tints the oak leaf
i seek the never bridled unspurred ponies
that gallop through beach sand and splash through tears
i listen to the voices coming from the lichen
covering the stones outcast from the sky
i search for the island where bleached conch shells
are washed up from graves of indians who worshipped the firefly
i reach towards the maple leaves inside the owl's eye
as he flies through the green arms of water embracing the coral
i ask the insects hidden in the grasses to tell me
how to overcome the loathsome ways of man's civilization

22.

Memory returns to a
morning
in Florida
when I leaned
on a ditch bank
by a
slaughter house.

              At the back
a stream
        thick with brown scum
sluggishly
          trickling
                through
discarded bricks.
              A dead oak
with black buzzards
                on its
grey bare branhes.
Near my hands,
                pieces of
hair,
      parts of the slaughtered
cow's hide,
              dark brown,
spotted.

In front
          a deep rain puddle
between
          cabbage palms.
                      Snowy
egrets
      doing
          a
              mating
                    dance,
fluffy feathers
              leaping,
a landscape
            of mobile
whiteness.

23.

On a swamp's edge
a clearing,
            some scattered palmettos,
a shack,
            climatis vine growing on
the greyed and greened
                        cypress boards.
A bed made from
            raw boards,
                        hard,
shoulder aches.

A rusty frying pan.
            bent handle,
now
      holding finely woven pine needles,
a wren's nest.

            During the night, the stillness
the silence.
            From a dark pine
                        to a
dark pine
            a flying squuirrel.
                        Out
of the darkness,
            the call
                        of
                              a
chuck will
      and
            an
                  answer.

24.

In Tennessee
   from the mountain
forest
  the call
    of
     a
whippoorwill
   and
     an
       answer.

On the open
   stage
     a play
about human beings
      abusing
other human beings.

25.

As we rode
   to the
      plankchurch
funeral,
   backyard
     claymound
graveyard,
    old fruit jars,
sandy insides,
    faded
crepepaper covered, broken
rubber band sticking,
      marigold
stem filled,

          passed a swallow flock,
greenwinged,
        irregular patterns flying
putting
      Japanese brushstroke shadows
on greengold wheat.

26.

The bluewinged
         cinnamon
breasted
     swallow
        darts
into cave
      beneath
         the ledges.

The sumac hairy stems touch
my elbow
       into a new existence
created
      by the slaughtered
cow's hide.

27.

        Through the fog
a brown rock,
        seven cormorants
on rock,
     outstretched wings, a
feather missing.

          My body created
by free
     cormorants,
              not by
the man
     exploited
          cormorant,
a rope
     around his neck,
             being
forced
     to give a man
          his fish.

28.

     Below ledge
after ledge
       after spruce
pines firs birch
         a house
built
     to resemble
           something
in the Swiss Alps.
         A newsboy
riding
     up to the house.

Clytaemestra,
        ex cheer leader,
national beauty queen,
          chairman
of local censorship
          committee,
  who gave up her career
as an opera coloratura

          to
be an apartment wife
       and
rear
    her one child, Orestes,
drinks
     instant coffee,
        the
frozen process variety,
       with
Aegisthus,
     a sportswriter.

They plan carefully, notng
every item of expense, searching
discount catalogues to cut
down the cost, trying to decide
the type of murder that will be
the cheapest. Agamemnon
is coming home.

He, a lawyer and distinguished
civic leader, has been away
on vacation, carried his son
to Africa to murder leopards.
He believes that a family
that kills together stays together.

     Orestes
much to his father's disapproval,
especially
     after educating his son
on how to mix and drink cocktails,
being sure
     to get the right one
in the right glass,
      neglected

his social drinking
                  and became
high on pot,
               missed the airplane.

             Orestes
will come home
             later
and shoot
          his mother
with the same gun
             that
he shot the leopard.
His mother's and the
leopard's head
            will
stay close together
on the walls
           of his
real estate office.

Meanwhile
Clytaemestra and Aegisthus
read the morning paper:

most secure base
                 attacked
weekend wound up
                by a trip
police search
            for a girl's body
an attack
            in drugstore parking lot
disorderly conduct
               unbecoming
a man wearing a
            gorilla suit

fires burned
          more than
eighteen hours
               the fuel
destroyed
          was valued
                    reduces
possession of five
               grams or
less
     from felony
               autopsies
were conducted
               on
                    316
avoid the obvious
               you find
of breaking
          through red
tape
     weight control
                         at west
point they believe in
motherhood
          sixty year old
woman
     attacked
               one eye
knocked out
          breaks leg
at beauty contest
               i got
no pleasure
          out of
exposing
     his
          wrong

doings
         picasso statue
attacked
         anyone
who wishes may make
a donation
              firebase
attacked
         twenty-two
miles
      per gallon
unidentified man
                    attacks
couple
      sleeping in park
dummy
      followed
              with
                  a
deuce
      a counterattack
Paul VI
      cabled the
distraught villagers
                 your
property is described as
         lots no 41 and 42
         block 1804 in unit 45
                  they did not
find his child
              after the
attack
      broken and twisted
wood
      in one street
i flew my private plane
people had been
                 warned
to stay out
            in the open

29.

My legs touched
                by a
needle,
        a green needle,
a green wood
                needle,
a creeping
        juniper
                needle.

30.

Charles Ives
                never read
newspapers
                A friend told him
about
        Hitler
                Ives wrote to
Roosevelt

31.

                American bulldozers
uprooting
        the Boi Loi
                woods

These distant woods
                unconcerned
                with human concerns
                but becoming
                concerned in

                              our
                              theirs
                              or someone's
                              or no one's
                              concern

Trees
        being
                destroyed
to protect
                a
                     man
                              from
a
    man

man the excresence

Trees destroyed
leaf bark limb root beginnings
destroyed
the consciousness beginnings
destroyed
pulled from the earth
to rot
into other words
other beginnings
rooting to create
a different body
from the body
that had its
consciousness begun
in leaf bark limb root

Trees destroyed
other beginnings to create
the future bodies:

tossed rocks tearing open
a three year old boy's mouth
torch thrown to burn
pigs goats geese
trench knife peeling off
an old woman's skin
a steelwool polished bayonet
cutting a man into strips

32.

Boi Loi woods
             you are no longer
present
       but your death is present
in every eye
          every eye creating another
eye
   and being created
             in that creation
of the other eye

          Boi Loi woods
before you died
your death
         was present
         in the bullet
         whistling
         a dirty song
         from a
         Texas tower

         The bullet
         from the Texas Tower
         was created
         by an ambassador
         killing for entertainment

a kudo
The bullet
was loaded
in the rifle
by a lawyer
who takes
his son
to Africa
to kill leopards

33.

Boi Loi woods
               your death
was planned
               by the hand
adjusting the forked stick
to level
          the buffalo gun

your death
           was planned
by the rancher's bank account
shotgunning
           the prairie dog

your death was planned
by the extinction of
the ferret's sharp face
your death was planned
by the badger's broken leg
as he limps
           through the thick
steak
    served
        after
           onion soup

to fifth rate
      violin
         music
played by a flesh colored corpse
standing
    in
       front
          of
            white
curtains

34.

Boi Loi woods
        your death
will be our
      death

Our death
      already present
in the words
     firing
from a snow bus
from an airplane
from snow shoes
       to murder
wolves
    the musicians
    the poets
    of solitary places

        the same hand
        that shoots
        the wolf
        is another hand
        from the
        same body

that murders
the eagle
the coyote
the cougar
the bobcat
the alligator
that clubs for profit
the baby seal
is another hand
from the body
that peels
off an
old woman's skin
is the hand
throwing the rocks
to tear open
the child's mouth
is the hand
that shoots sharks
that shoots wood ducks
that shoots quail
is the hand
of the fake poet
who carries
a bow and arrow
to kill an animal
and then
pretends
he is
some kind
of mystic
by putting
the animal's head
on his
pitiable head
is the same hand
that cuts open

the screen
rapes
and knocks out
the eye
of a seventy year
old woman
is the same hand
that after patting
his son on the head
aims the
Christmas gift
and murders
a circling hawk
is the same hand
that slices
open the stomach
of an old man
and sticks
a flag
in his intestines

35.

The wolf
whose howls
barks
yelps
    are a tragic poetry
            as great
as King Lear
      The wolf is
as great a poet as Shakespeare
He has only
    to howl

36.

The last howl
              from the
bleeding body
              of the wolf
the last wolf
              gathers
puts together
              the bricks
for the furnaces
in the concentration camps
of the
       future

37.

              Once more
the quick dart
              of the bluewinged
swallow
       into the cave
                     beneath
the ledges,
              into the dark
interior
       of the cliff.

              I leave
the path,
       step onto
                 the
slippery
       ledges,
              the dark

steps downward,
                    steps
darkened
          by touches
                    from
the hands of the ocean.
This place,
          ledge after ledge,
is called
          the shatter zone, the
ancient zone
                    of fragmentation, the
region
          of the cracked
                    the disjoined
where illusions of solidarity
                    and
cohesion
          are
                broken
                    into
sharp pointed pieces.

                    Once
always
          forever
                daily
                    threatened
with destruction
                being
                    shattered,
scattered
          and rescattered,
                    a chaos.

But a granitic substance
                    created by

a solitary imagination
a gull's shadow
A painted brown dog
A turtle's back
a wolf's howl
a leopard's spots
the swallow's flight

a granitic substance
  formed
      from
         the
           bodies
of a few
    a solitary man
    standing on one foot
    on hot desert sand
    kissing
    the flesh of the wind
    after departure from
    the photographs
    devouring landscapes

a granitic substance
        that
           resorted
and consolidated
      a
        rock

38.

                              i
go
      into
              the sadness
                              of
the
      eyeless
              fish
that swim
              in the one
sand grain
              i
                  hold

MUD ON THE STREETS

I press
my hands
hard against
a pile
of fallen
pine needles
until I
feel a
brown river
depositing
mud
on the streets.

THE SUBMERGED FERN IN THE WAISTLINE OF SOLITUDE

I

Inside the dead night heron's eye
sinking into angular shadows
left by the cement fingers, the bottled moon
rests on the shelf shaping
with its light the leash and the tatter.
Nailed to the bird's skullbones
the yellow light surrounding
an island of washbowls, the surf
spotted with the closed shutters of morning,
the dove wings of blood vessels
flapping suicidal starlight on blueprinted faces,
and the top of the stairs
dragging artificial soundless bells
to load the empty ropes
hanging from the rafters in eyeballs.
A finger touches the drill point
carried in the turning teeth of merry-go-round horses,
and the drilled hole is stuffed
with charts of multiplication tables
printed across the spines of barebacked blue notebooks.

Mango trees, coffee plants, song sparrows
glitter in the light sticking a pincer
through a crack in the long necked bottle.
Sleep has paralyzed the dictionary and the wind
cannot open its pages.
The wrecking bar carried in the fists
of keys to the asbestos inside barbed fences
is pecked apart by nighttime orchids.

II

Flowers going under anesthesia
as the mushrooms pop up in the sky's damp spots.
Sponges safe in an ocean of sharks
lift the cloth off the butterflies'
memories of golden caterpillars
chewing away the sleeves of whitewashed straitjackets.

Foottracks still walking through the seaweed
growing in the wood grains of these floorboards
sawed from the feathers of dark rains
jumping from the fifteenth story of the plate glass cloud.
The earthworm seeks the earthworm of the hoe's nightmare,
twists out from the closed hands of the office rug,
falling into the foam at the tip of a needle.

The face stuck in a wash basin of razors,
as the bays and the oceans next to the white island
change metal into the cactus' momentary yellow flower.
The thermometer between the stone's lips
climbs the red vines towards the stained glass window
where the lambs are shot by the arrows of dress suits.
The fever was left in the bicycle wheels of fantasies
whose rims pushed the buttons of automatic elevators
rising towards the floor of the buried bread.
From the balconies by the black windows
the left hands unscrew the fingers from the right hands
and toss them to the victor standing in his nightclothes.
The children wearing rubber gloves dance
around the broken wing of a tear
struggling to crawl away and hide in the gauze
wrapped around the healthy lungs
leaning against the outsides of stucco drugstores.

III

The insults from the houses buried under carnivals
push the raincoat towards the raincoat.
The titles on the bottom of the bags of roaches
chase the shoulder to touch the shoulder.
The jail waving a duck at an unborn taxi
prepares for the sandspurs to break through the rotten saddle.

In the chrysalis hanging on the elm
the waters embrace the waters.

IV

The legendary salt buried in cemeteries
will not stay hair and bones
but must sleepwalk down driveways
and wave to the slot machines flying over the ocean.
The empty net, the empty crate, the empty cage
rot and collapse among empty pajamas.
Out from the crumbling bars sprout
the snails and their bright yellow twisted homes.

Climbing concealed ladders to peep
through the cracks in the eye of the bird
those who have carved their initials
down the spines of grapes, stars, and doves.
Asylums dripping from their mouths
dampen the tablecloths spread over tunnels.
Ashes from the bottom of stakes
are repainted silver and pasted
along the edges of awards and diplomas.

Customs have no spiderwebs and spin their traps
throughout the metal of caution signs.
The one way street flares with headlights
coming from the wrong direction.
Behind the planked-up eyes cats play in the parlor corn stalks.

Walking down the path between
the buried sounds of bent clarinets
towards the sifted flour falling on leaves
the day loses its bruised legs
and stands upright in the secrets of coral,
and the thorns of rivers tack closed
the door to the lichened covered stone hammers.

V

In the curtained water where the chained eels
spit out marked highways
the drowned man grips the anchor.
His eyes lost and enclosed in milk cartons
floating by the dead frogs in canals.
He is satisfied to feel the petals of the invisible rose.
Headphones riveted to his ears he hears
pocket watches clicking in bank buildings
and the vanished waters of mirages
sloshing in buckets on the outskirts of his sleeve.
He has never stood inside the eye of the dead bird.

There is the distance that destroys
the object in between.
Between the doorknob and the telephone pole
the moth on the milkweed.
A desk's small space has wrecked rooms of water
to overflow and flood the dragonflies' whispered wings.

An anatomy with a painted ceiling: moons, both near
and far sighted, shining on a transparent girl
in the show windows of a hermetic drugstore, a man
dressed in a suit of bitten fingernails slapping
the dirty heads sticking out from cries of pain,
two men under a spotlight exchange packages of shoulder blades,
a chisel made from eyelashes glued together with fellowship
cuts two thousand years ino an eyeshadowed calculating machine,
twelve men in flare bottom trousers kneel and spread
fish bones on the road coming from the beaded door.

VI

The offers: the stitched eyelids of the silver pitcher,
the wrong names to write under the portraits of pears,
desires counted on the fingers of the severed hand,
kisses from chalkmarks scribbled on the sidewalk,
scissors to cut the long hair of the lightning.

A hay barn, a silo, and a moon printed under dresses,
a bottle of beer with the fingerprints of a boatyard,
the self confidence that comes from sleeping
in switched on chairs along the deck railings
of a saint's tomb steaming towards the West Indies
and searching for a shorter route to the electric silk
that will stroke the stigmata cut on the chest
by a pocketbook stuffed with insured credit cards.

VII

A look at the wood of the table, the knowledge
the tree is gone forever. A century ago a seed
where now a road of anonymous housebroken coins
travel rapidly towards blood drops on oil tanks,
where footprints have no bodies and hoe
straight rows in the gardens with false dirt.

The destruction of the hand leaves the hand's shadow
around the wings of the canary paralyzed on a bank rug.
All gates are nailed closed by the white beards
who wave during the late hours to nonexistent taxis
and hold in their caresses sacks of horizons made from gymnasiums.
The wrecking bar that pulls a rotten voice
from a body destroys the midnight in a cave's tear.

Inside the eye of the dead night heron
touch the algae that floats on mirrors after long rains
touch the seafoam on the shoulders of naked shells
touch the submerged fern in the waistline of solitude.

THE HOLY SANDSPUR

i
   heard
        an unknown
bird song

        started
in its
      direction

arrived
       at a spot of
charred pine branches
foottracks across ashes

at my feet
         sandspurs
i kneeled
      noticed
each sandspur
        has a
reddish
     tint
       running
up
  its
    holy
      spire

IRONIC BEAVER

There was a road darkened by Australian pines.
I dreamed the road had no beginning,
and when I came to the end's white space,
there would be no feeling I had left anything.
On my desk the ironic beaver
on the back of a Canadian nickel
crawled off the metal.
He carried in his teeth the road's origin.
A dam was built in my blood
blocking the flow, leaving a space of mud
on which there was an indentation
where a dead bird had sunk into the earth.

DAPHNE

Now we have met
both by the warm gulf and the cold ocean
knowing we
will never part from one another
knowing we
will always be separated
knowing you will be whole
only when my imagination
stitches together
the scattered pieces of your body
arms eyelashes legs
leaf roots bark
Knowing I will exist
only when you exist
only when
the white pine by the green water
becomes you

When the bark becomes your breast
the leaves your hair
the branches your arms
the treetop your face
when during those rare moments
the sand around your roots breathes
when you tree are Daphne

Never as Apollo
will
I try to impose order
by arranging your disordered hair
Never will I repeat Apollo's words:
"What if your hair were properly arranged"
but will let
your disorder
arrange me
arrange the wrinkles in my face
and I will let my face
arrange the wrinkles in the sand along the shoreline

THE GULF HAS SPOKEN TO YOU

The gulf has spoken to me
The sea oats have spoken to you

The dead morning glory vine blows down the beach
speaking its last words

You refuse to listen
Your ears rest in the bottoms of your pockets
You reach around them to feel bank deposits

Now speaks the sand in the cement holding up your houses
It is less gentle more angry
shouting that your deafness will not save you

A LOVE POEM

Gone are the fourteen lined love sonnets
in which
Sydney declared his allegiance to politics
and Shakespeare
as Fiedler would have all American novelists
to male friendship
except in the last few
an elementary not very friendly passion
of a man something other than profound or humanized

Iambs have rusted away with other outmoded machines
Now to express love requires control of your breath

What fragment of breath
                 can give
                     love
                           to these words
a measured two
              followed by
                      these separated ones

                      the urge the urge
                      to be a fashion
                      to continue
                      in this
                      two-one-one-one
                      interrupted
                      by a two one
                      to become
                      an engineer of breath

to quote a physicist   express the deepest feeling by
a reference to Quericke's experiments with Magdeburg
hemispheres   Add some Latin: *Materia vincor et quia*
lingua minor   mention an orbit copy a sentence
from a Marboro bargain book on Egyptian mythology
do a buffalo dance   do a ghost dance do a silverfox foxtrot

Tonight we
although
it is not night
it is morning
but we cannot
say morning
for morning
requires
the unemotive
breath

        Time does
        not
        belong
        to the clock
        but
        to the stone

the wind's voice in the antelope gallop of the stone's surface
is the time we reach out to hold the time in the hand we touch

Rilke Krolow Celan
        knew more about love than the extension
and retraction of their lungs
        wir schlafen wie wein
        in den Muscheln

        we can
        we must
        first
        we must
        abolish
        we should
        then abolish
        we must
        to become
        we are
        then
        we is

we are the lightning darting from the lizard's eye
as the lizard darts from the crumbled brown red rock
into the dark green of the lonely bush struggling
from a land of brown red crumbled rock

       We are the oak tree's shadow
       we are the sunlit grass not shadowed
       we are the small oak
       with the backlit leaves
       we are the dark leaves
       of the distant oak
       we are the dark leaves
       of the nearby dying oak

All we know is that we will not go to New York City
this summer even if Gobbi comes to sing in Figaro

       we will walk
       through a field
       listen
       to a
       black snake sing

our touch our field touch our black snake singing touch
our walking touch recreates the cracked apple's green
of a chinese vase we are the white broken plum branch
touching a black sky   we are the sacred blue eye   the
ivory uplifted hand saying i intervene   we are inside
a glass case denting the yellow cloth   we are burgundy
wine drunk in front of neptune   we are the white pekingese
turning his back on the crowd   we are the stolen
tabby marked brown persian cat   we are the rainbows
on the sugarbird's wings   we are the stone dog
at the stone knight's foot   we are a pinpoint of light
on a pitcher in vermeer   the close of a mahler symphony

IMMANENTIST SUTRAS

AN EXPLICATION OF THE PHILOSOPHY BEHIND IMMANENTISM AS BELIEVED ON MAY 28ᵗʰ, 1973

this is a poetry without beards   even without
a commune of chins or dynamite   it is buried
in a mountain and does not accept the gift waves
from the squeaks of a donkey cart   the shovel
is its brother and its enemy   it accepts the
sea grape leaf on the illusory path and the
yellow dot suspended in the air   this
introduction is a variant on the door who
requires a key and a key's grandfather and then
requires the key to become invisible and swim
through the blade of a sword   it is a dove
who was painted on bricks and began to fly
until someone asked permission   immanentism
is a muzzle becoming a horse and a chain
becoming raw ore it finds the shadow of a fly
to be as great as the fly and greater than
the fly swatter or congress it takes the
fever from the earth and puts it in its proper
place   because most people can count to ten
we refuse to count past zero and we also refuse
to count minus numbers   we have seen scarecrows
run away at the sight of a mustache and we
know in what coat linings the scars and their
starlight are hidden   doors belong in other
vocabularies

IMMANENTIST SUTRAS

I.

The flame separated from its lamp
kneels to lap up the sun
Its waters of fire and the thirst in the hand
The extinguished bark is soft inside the blood
The tree lives in the rainbow
At the point day becomes night
the lightning will give the tree a new leaf

II.

The charred wick rubs against the fence
The smear on the bleached bone
holds a spool of thread made from eyelashes
The faces built from fallen shingles
deny the original trees
The white radiant skeleton
observes his former skin
become a tent for raindrops

III.

On the bank the thick stiff hair
of the hide skinned from slaughtered stars
The stars' eyes run away
and hide in burrows beneath burned fields
Their bones increase the thirst of floating roots
You give your skin to warm their cold hair
Already the sand becomes transparent

IV.

The fur scraped across the eye
unknown to the steel sun
The metal eyeball escapes the stretched arm's blood
The wind's roots blow in the opposite direction
The scraped eye awakens the burned paper beneath the rock
The wind's stem and leaf is your bridge

V.

The memory of the broken rope
and the memory of the brown house
cannot be called a fist or open hand
They touch the footprint inside quartz
The indentation made by a bare foot without weight
One need not ask when
the past action leaves the stone
to circle the present orange leaf
The given light is a wave
sunken under the wet board
It has become the body of the curled worm
All is explained
by the speech now
heard from the distant dark oak
who lifts her body out of a star
The twisted roots are the hair
of the absent and everpresent night

VI.

The stuffed crow on the mast of the glass ship
The light from the eye falls stumbles limps
towards the dead sun and the dead body
The paper sun and the paper body breathe
Their ashes chop off the light
and chop off the flesh
The new sun scatters itself
over the buried grass in the snowland
The new body touches the hand of a leaf

VII.

With the light from the ignition of the pebble
ignited by the caw left in the air by the flown crow
the recognition of the dislocated jaw
The fire in the body warms and desires no ash
A line up of ash smeared faces dissolves
and the mist is grabbed by the old man
greedy for the ownership of space
The indestructible body is found in the fern
Our skins shine on the snails in the grasses
Clocks try to measure us.

VIII.

The shriveled hand places the sun in the center
Inside the astronomer's flesh
a bellringer pulls an empty bell
In the other cosmos
we turn an apparition into the apparition
change the thread pulled from the sweater
back into a grazing sheep
We see the transformation of grass
inside the transparent sheep
and through his transparent wool
we see the clay colored pond and the barbed fence
The new sheep becomes the true mirror
Our bodies stay on the silver glass
when we depart to hold baskets
The airplanes depart and arrive
according to our breath misty on the surface
The sun moves around our reflection

IX.

When the body is found in the fern
the fern knows it does not own the body
and the body knows it does not own the fern
Ownership exists in the other space
where the old man dyes his hair
Now who is and who is here
is a raindrop not yet fallen
and is turning into a green stem
who is a finger on the luminous hand
who touches the sun beneath the roots

X.

The pulsations in the fern
move inside the arm
The breath is inside the bark
fallen from the oak
The heart gives and receives
from the blood streams in the sandgrains
The raindrop containing the eyes
sinks into the ocean
inside the banana blossom
The vanished hands hold the sun

XI.

Eyes tired from pulling the weight of the illusory stone
collapse before the diagram of the pyramid
The old man with a rope made from his eyelashes
beats the back of the wind
The red marks create the cyclone's skin
Those who follow the old man
whittle the stars to dust
In a futile attempt to carve
heads for their headless bodies
The cyclone walks down the sidewalk
and holds a lamp whose flame is utter darkness

XII.

The old man bewildered among his scissors
We unravel the stitches from our eyelids
and open our eyes to see the darkness
not the darkness before the light
not the dark night of the soul
but darkness who is light
and the light who is darkness
and the light-darkness who is our bodies
Without a sun the moon glows in our blood
We touch the shell without edges or middle
the olive shell who crawls
under the sand in our bones

XIII.

The swallow has a body made of sky
and the sky flies through itself
The street signs and the house numbers
become meaningless
The old voices clamped to the brain
fall down in a swoon
and nibble on the edge of a bowl
that contains dark oranges
The glowworm and the turtle
become our companions
and guide us through the paralyzed stars

XIV.

In a landscape of mirrors the cufflinks
glisten under the electric light
The heads nod in accord
with the gears and pulleys
that moisten the dust of the dead old man
Slender and rough fingers
rub the warmth from the top
of his gold grave
Mirrors smash against mirrors
Each broken piece is kissed and rekissed

XV.

In the memory beyond memory
the fern becomes our spinal cord
Green impulses whisper through our bodies
They become the source of the rain
who falls inside our brains
Our bones become soaked in green light
The emanations from our bodies
grow lichens on the loneliness of stones

THE POEMS OF DUANE LOCKE

THE WORD

Word, when I find you,
under the leaf, under the stone,
under the barnacle covered driftwood,
I gaze at your birth.
The sun and moon carved from card tables
hide in the caves on the steep side of the wind.
There is the cry, the smile,
and the circling of the seagull.
Yours is a strange birth,
for you were not born young, but old,
and you must become invisible before sight can begin.
Your first task is to remove your clothes,
for you were born fully clothed.
As you unbutton the definitions that cover you
and start to breathe,
I hear forgotten things;
the sun that shines inside the skin
of the clam shell stuck upright in the mud,
the chips of cypress bark that float on a dark pond.
As I listen, my listening causes you to grow smaller.
Starfish replace the acetylene torches in the sky,
and soon I do not know the sky or you.
You have gone beyond the limitations
of roads, bridges, and iron oranges,
and have become enclosed
in the infinity of the sand dune.
Now I feel your fingers on the top of my hand
as I utter you.

LIFE IMITATES ART

Life imitates art. I think
of Jules Supervielle still damp
from the Uruguay sea
at Oloran Sainte Marie,
and Valéry, dry and remote,
at his cemetery by the sea.
I drive down the rain of the moon,
past long stretches of barbed night.
A kingbird who chased all other birds away
has gone to sleep in a cloud.
The black angus huddle together
and lick the salt from fallen stars.
The white plank church slowly sinks
into the crickets' sound.
I walk towards a stone where algae
has changed a grey name to green.
An empty jar wrapped in tinfoil
looks up at a sky of wilted marigolds.
I keep hearing a toy telephone ring,
the one you bought me long ago on a train.
I have answered it many times,
but no voice came out the other end.
Now I understand the meaning of the bent thimble
that I never removed from the warped drawer.
I was trying to keep your thumb alive.

WE ARE ON ANOTHER SHORE

It has been proven that goats
at the time of crowded hallways
graze on frozen starlight, but it is not stated by
the bronze tinted eyelashes that are pasted on pages.
When we have hoofs and elicit the horror
of coathangers and chalk dust,
and drink the light that flows
from the wounded side of the orange
and float inside the mud sealed hollow logs
in a sky of bears that sprouts between oak roots,
we shift from the shape of the loon to the shape of the otter,
and dive into the coral we have spoken.
The owners of binderies and collators
set their alarms and touch
the dead roosters in their vest pockets,
and tack the skin of the tiger
on the side of closed gas stations.
We are on another shore
where sea turtles bury their eggs in our vocabularies.

A BELATED INSIGHT: A LAMENT FOR A USELESS EDUCATION THAT STRESSED CONCEPTUAL THOUGHT AND PRACTICAL NECESSITY

If you can only rid yourselves of conceptual thought,
you will have accomplished everything.

— Huang Po

Language now occupies the place once occupied by the gods
or some other external entity or outward thing.

— Octavio Paz

The fields gather in the hidden places
where the bones inside our bodies meet,
as if the bodies' other parts
were their enemies.
Fires and cutting machines are
the expectations of their daily existence.
How can we tell them
they can live without harm
inside our blood
and never be destroyed by our nerves.
How can we
talk
to the wheat, the straw, the goldenrod
that breathe inside our bodies.
We were taught a useless language,
practical, theoretical,
and we were never taught
to speak their language.
We cannot talk to these inner fields;
we are helpless before their fear,
as helpless as before
the ignorance of the professor,
who has not the least comprehension
of the modern poem, or any poem,
or the lizard, the iguana, or the salamander.
Our past was put on his lathe
and he held his illusions in his steady hand
and reshaped our bodies
to resemble his stillborn foetus.

He pressed dead goldfinches
in his grammar book
and sought the flower in the sky
by standing in front of mirrors.
We can speak his language
because he taught us his language,
and we find ourselves
shut off
from the wheat fields
that grow out of our bones.
If we had only been intelligent enough
to understand the misdirections of Western man,
he might have saved us from his language,
and then tonight
our conversation
would have been
with the unborn wheat.

WU-WEI

Few understand me
        — Lao-tzu

*At such moments, the store of knowledge so painfully gathered at
school and university strikes me as a largely worthless clutter of facts
and shallow views that lead to the fritting away of one's life on vain
pursuits.*
        — John Blofeld

Today
by this crystal water,
in this clean place,
transparent
to reveal
the thousand blazing eyes
of the purple underwater plant,
transparent
to reveal
the holy motion
of the fins
on the blue spotted fish,
today
by the source
of the dying river,
I shall live
as the light
around the edge
of the avocado leaf,
I will change
as the light changes,
but I know
as I altar
from darkness to light
and light to darkness
the demons
with the plaster masks
of a faked Apollo

over their
illusory faces,
the demons who wear
white laboratory robes
and carry in their hands
paralyzed in the shapes of gloves
the frog's backbone,
atomic numbers, and dust
stolen from the moon,
these demons
will come
and try to gouge
out my eyes
and replace my eyes
with a slide rule
and two piles
of blue sawdust,
but today
as I am the light
around the edge
of the avocado leaf
I live a life
these demons
can never understand
and will be baffled
on how to begin
their disfigurement,
they will not know
where to stick their needles
and therefore
their ignorance
renders this one day
safe from their destruction,
and I can live safely
as the light
around the edge

of the avocado leaf,
and I can listen
to the primordial
wren's song
from the ancient cedar
in the center
of the sun.

LOBSANG DORJE CHANG

Experience of a radically desacralized nature is a recent discovery;
moreover, it is an experience accessible only to a minority in modern
society, especially to scientists. For others, nature still exhibits a charm,
a mystery, a majesty in which it is possible to decipher traces of ancient
religious value.

—Mircea Eliade

All afternoon
I had been asleep
by hoofprints
filled with spotted water.
My head rested on
matted pine needles,

and when I awoke
I saw a backlit leaf
spin down
from a gum tree,
and three yellow
mushrooms,
each rimmed
with a soft light.
I turned over
to find a patch
of pitcher plants
with a single
thick white
starshaped flower.
This afternoon,
I will break a habit
and not meditate
on Lobsang Dorje Chang.

THE LONG STRAIGHT SHADOWS BARK
AT BUTTERFLIES

I, separated from the words inside telephone wires,
watch the long straight shadows bark at butterflies.
You, stiff brown leaf, a second of sunlight on a dried stem,
suddenly depart, and stand under gum trees, a clay water creek
with frog's eyes, a web of starlight woven between the
burning blouse of the hairdresser and the wet
electricity of the rainbow colored squid.

WE HAVE CEASED LOOKING FOR SIGNS

We have ceased looking for signs
in this landscape of battered doves
Each feather a menace to the egg
Each crack a fixture on the wall
What crawls on the grass
was drowned before flight

I am watched by cabbages and closed eyes
My hand is stamped by the cactus blossom
waiting in the root
The yucca has my hand in its height
The turned away backs uplift
the fallen leaf to the vine

I am not seen when looked at
The ocean in the stone
sends its waves over my face
I taste salt on my lips
The hair of the snow has frozen my hand
I have forgotten what it says on my doorplate

I lean against the rain
I must comprehend the thoughts of scattered bones
Fur grows on the fins
I leave the marble patio
and its pictures of smoky urns.

AFTER A DREAM
ABOUT THE YELLOW EMPEROR
AND HIS THREE IMMORTAL LADIES

Through the rocks
shaped like snorting horses
the trail walked.
Ahead a dazzling green expanse of light.
I could not tell
where the thick bamboo ended
and the green temple began.
Crossed the wooden jetty
and heard
the minnows' voices.
Each voice was the voice
that spoke the words
I always believed I had spoken
but actually never had spoken,
but now one
with the minnows
I was speaking these words
and my fins
serenely moved through the wind.

AN ECLIPSE OF CUT HAIR

You, the roots of rain
that burrow through the beginnings of coal
until during an eclipse of cut hair
you are born in a bay bush as a wren
now fly as a word across the buried frost.

Word close to me, pressed
against the mosses, the lichen, and the cypresses
that are my body,
I see your foottracks
suddenly appear in a lengthening row over the sun
and drop off to darken the black sky of the moon.

I speak the space you left
on the golden pond
where the salamander slid
under the crossed dead leaves.

At night I study nails.

PARAVRITTI

Paravritti: *turning back up the energies of the subtle body which are normally wasted in daily perception and action.*

—from *The Art of Tantra* by Philip Rawson

A crowd:	Where did you go this summer?
A person:	The summer pulled water from a star.
A crowd:	You went to that place the summer before.
A person:	The twist of the air was the entry into the river under the star.
A crowd:	Don't you get tired of always going to the same place?
A person:	The hay as it grows older becomes grass and sends its roots through the moon.
A crowd:	I never liked that place.
A person:	The eyelashes on the grape turned to rain when the fish flew through the tree.
A crowd:	How much did your vacation cost?
A person:	When I put my finger through the sky I touched a furry sand grain.
A crowd:	Did you borrow the money?
A person:	A buffalo was perched on the hair of a comet and he held a diamond.
A crowd:	Now you will have to spend the rest of the year paying it back.

BEETLE

In memory of Pablo Neruda and his un escarabajo

Beetle, I watch you
crawl
from the black earth,
from the open spot
between dying leaves,
the spot
scratched by a claw,
this place
where the armadillo
buried my name.

I have often heard
this space,
this disturbed earth,
this piece of damp dirt
tap at night
on my window sill.

Beetle, open my door
and let my name
without leaving
the earth
enter the room.

Beetle, bring me
the black rainbow
and the river
on your hard wings.

Let the thorns
on your legs
circle the brow
of my breath
and awaken
the feathers
and fur
inside my chest.

Beetle, take the sky
out of my backpocket
and put it in my hand.

WHEN I DECIDED TO BE BORN

When I decided to be born
I asked the moon
to let me be born
on a dark night
when the corn's eyes
were open.

I asked the hard clay earth
under the long porch
to have me born
in an unpainted room
with a broken window
that could not be closed
and would let my cries
go outside
and touch the walnuts.

I asked an old star
about to fall
before it fell
to put an owl
in the walnut tree
and let the owl scream
to his mate
until his scream
crossed out the moon.

Then I asked the wheat
to tell the wild fox
who hid in the wheat
never to be afraid of me,
to come out in the open
raise up his head
and let his howl
give me hope
by changing the voice
of the wind.

THE GEORGIA LANDSCAPE GAVE ME LIFE

The pines, the sycamores, the chinaberries,
the gums, and the oaks
were still there when I was born.
And the moon and the sun and the stars
solidified in the bright wood beneath the bark
came out of the bark and formed my bones.
The pigs, the cows, and the one white horse
sent vibrations through the air to give me flesh.
Scents from fallen pine branches walked from the woods
through the glistening wheat fields
to touch a formless mass into the shape of my nose,
sounds from peacocks and guinea hens created my ears,
taste was given me by the wild grape, the wild blackberry,
and the shaggy pomegranate tree near the rusty dinner bell.
My fingers came into being when my preexistence
walked between rows and touched
the rough husks, the moist white and purple flowers,
the intense softness of the cotton.
Finally on December the twenty ninth an indigo bunting
came out of the honeysuckle tangled over a ditch
and said, "Let him be born."

In my present room surrounded by wires
and meaningless voices traveling through the wires,
the clay that after a rain sticks between the bare toes
rocks in an old chair
a long black shawl covers its grey hair
and it knits
fireflies on the dark.

THE DISCOVERY OF ASIA:
YANG—YIN OR YAB—YUM

But for the primitive, such an act is never simply physiological; it is,
or can become, a sacrament, that is, a communion with the sacred.

— Mircea Eliade

They try to decide on what ceremony, what manual.
Perhaps a tantric ritual. Open the ice box,
turn up the air conditioner, shake
ice cubes on the rug, and they can
pretend they are in the Himalayas.
What ever happened to those red
chickens, the old stone wall,
and the sadness of the rural scene.
It was only last summer, they chilled
the wine, and invited a goldfinch
to dinner. Perhaps what is wrong is
they both learned how to read. If one
had been illiterate, he could have been
exploited by the other, and they would
have had a happy symbiosis.
They decide to turn back on the lights
and read a book about Paul and Virginia.

THE GRAND PROSTRATION

All the gurus we hired
have lost their fingernails.
Their pranayama had not the
proper credentials
to contain the calcium.
In the basement rented
by the bearded schoolteacher
and converted by a charcoal Buddha,
we swore to each other
that we had found enlightenment
and now were on a rooftop
above all good and evil,
but still we got arrested
when we parked overtime
and our tantra cound not
convince the jury.
Tonight as my legs ache
in this position
of the highest meditation
my mind's one point
begins to scatter
and brings back
my two divorces, unknown children,
and all my regrets.
Suppose I had
sent roses wrapped in wax paper,
or had gone ahead
and paid the back rent.

ANGELS

The other day I met an old man
who had spnt his entire life
rocking in a chair.
He whittled angels out of broomsticks
until he had so many angels
he had to move to a larger house.
The old man said to me,
"If one has lived a fulfilled life,
he does not mind dying."
I did not reply, but watched
this old man move his knife through wood.
I noticed how he enjoyed
the odor of the wood's blood,
and even his rocking chair
felt delight as it crushed the woodchips.

MAYPOP

At this wheat field's edge,
rain eroded, a bare red,
a dead blackberry, a wilted passion flower vine,
I see the disembodied touch of an old hand,
a hand that lifted the passion flowers,
but now this hand is named under bronze.
Yesterday while it rained I discussed immortality
in front of a lunch room;
the discussion was friendly,
it was with my worst enemy,
a man who stole hours from eight years of my life,
the man, whom you never saw, the man who caused
your hand to become arthritic.
As I stare at this gully
and at the dead vine's twisted fingers,
I hear you and your dog's footsteps
by this "maypop," the name
the starved children in your one room school
who had no other food in their lunch box
gave to this plant with the center cross.

A SEPARATE REALITY

The large black iron pot
and its price tag
from the antique shop
is now the piece de resistance
in your dying room,
once was other than a medicine
and a decoration,
more than a unique last joke.
Reddened hands
poured in potash
and chased away
the chickens pecking
around the red worms
that crawled through the coals.
I cannot explain
to your reflection
left on the glass
of your illusion collection
the washed flour sacks
I wore as baby dresses
when my cries were picked up
by blackbirds
and carried to the uncut pines.

PLOWSHARE

The plow rusts
under planks
crisscrossed by chance
and crumbling
according to fate.
The handle
has already joined
in death
the hands it held.
The emptiness
where the fingernails
broke the wood
was the last
to go,
for its heart was strong
and it screamed
for days
under the bed straps.
The steel and its rust
cannot remember
what was once
in the open space.

ALLEYS

I walk down alleys,
for there is a solitude in alleys,
not found on sidewalks.
There is a sacredness about alleys.
Often I find a companionship in chairs
that have been thrown away.
I converse with their cracked leather
and the wood where the paint is scraped off.
The chairs now quite as sad
as when they were houses.
We often talk about the old times
when their wood fused into the forest,
and when their roots
pumped the stars' voices
through their bodies.

A BLUE BIRD WHO FLEW
OUT OF A FENCE POST HOLE
AND PAUSED ON A PINE

not the origin, its unbornness,
but the birth, its embodiment,
the rare moment of the feather,
the birth cries of the sky and the grasses,
the blaze of the blue wing,
the close contact with the new sun,
the word being born from the flash,
your body being born from the word,
your body the unique word with no definition,
the post, the flight, the pause, the pine, the sun,
words without meanings and graves,
words living in the coral
of the flying and pausing word.

THE MICROSCOPES THAT ANCHOR
SAILBOATS NEAR CASINOS

I hear the iceberg in the trunk compartment
of an abandoned automobile call to stumps
scattered over the microscopes
that anchor sailboats near casinos.

You were not present in the knife marks
caught in the nets made from melted banks,
or in the twisted arm of the condemned tissue paper
enticed from the lunch stand that stayed open all night.
The pictures said to be you,
the pictures passed under caps behind the cheers of the pump house
and passed over the crushed cups and lost bottles beneath
bleachers were pictures of that not you:
the beheaded bell and the pawned rope,
the outturned pockets and six yellow scraps of washed paper,
the wax fern and the dice inside the bottle.

You, the broken seaweed stacked by a winter wind
on the other shore, watched and illuminated
the gunpowder that spun around inside the bicycle tire.
Your unborn hair in the thistle
I spoke to the bee and to the goldfinch.

PHOENIX PARK

*This inner way leads into the mystery of Amoghasiddhi, in which
the inner and the outer world, the visible and the invisible, are
united, and in which the spiritual takes bodily shape, and the body
becomes an exponent of the spirit.*

—Lama Anagarike Govinda

a red leaf
inside a breathing tear

a heron perched
on an absent star

the horizon burrows
under fallen oranges

a plum blossom
walks in a green eye

tiger stripes
creep through a hollow log

the mushroom lights
the pathway for ashes

the emptied mind
swims with the lantern fish
of the deepest ocean
inside your bones
and goes in and out
of the sky's reefs

DAKINI

When the dakini brings her dark body
out of my body into this dark space,
no bodies, no space;
measured time is a myth for pyramid builders.
This is the moment when the boards of houses
take off their paint
and change back into trees,
when the steel of the saw
throws away its identification card
and reenters the earth,
when all the chemists
change back into alchemists
and bless the sacred metal,
when all men renounce steaks
and enter the cave of meditation
to live on a few bowls of rice for centuries.

Now at night
when the star
leaves the sky
to float upon
the rainwater
in the blue bowl
made of wind
and the waters
from underground rivers,
I pick up
its hair
and spread
the light
across my hand.

My skin
becomes transparent
and I watch
an old wheel
half buried

in clay
among stubble
rust away
to become
the iron
in the blood
of the new born
flickers in a nest
behind a chimney
that stands
without a house.

Now that
the past
that walks
in my blood
supports
the sky
and gives
the stars
feathers
and lets
the moon
cackle
as it pecks
the corn
of strange light
grown on
distant comets,
I no longer need
to be
consoled
by the
illusions
exchanged
in conversations.

I stand still
and remain silent
as the mirrors
people place
on others' faces
fall and leave
a community of skulls.
All life
begins
in this cemetery.

THE VARIOUS LIGHT

FLORIDA RAINS

These are the hot months of heavy rain:
the fish in streams under bridges
add upper floors to their houses,
the water puts on a brown robe,
goes on a pilgrimage towards a shrine of roots,
some drops soaked through deep sand
climb stairs of wood, fiber, sap,
watch the moon from a penthouse in a pine.
The rain gives some of the sky it carries
to cure the mallows' rheumatism;
the mallows stand up straight and leap.
The morning glories keep open their shutters;
in the music room the bees practice their dancing lessons.
The prickly pears put on broad brimmed hats
and light yellow torches.

PAOLO AND FRANCESCA

Paolo chained to an antique chair
embroidered with swans halberds
shoelaces pulled out of shoes
snails oysters sea slugs shell-less hermit crabs
grottos ivory legged centipedes
the door lock made of turned away faces
the door carved on the limp of a walking cane
Under mummy cloth of fist three moonlit scales
A clubbed seal slid inside his brain
Beheaded people wept by a horse's skeleton
Red cloaked men rode on bicycles painted like palomino horses
His sword climbed out of the tower
slashed open a bag of dyed hair
the hair turned grey and twisted itself into a rubber ball
bounced on a tight rope stretched between columns

Francesca broke the teeth of her black comb
Her hair climbed the vines of the wind
The moon covered itself with black ink
She pulled a crimson cord and rain fell on her pin cushion
She looked for fleas on the oranges in the crystal bowl
She ran down a long and narrow archway to a window
A wild poppy floated in the middle of the Arno
A painted magpie flew from the ceiling
She tied the door shut with the court clown's umbilical cord
A turban bled on her fingernails

Her husband who had no name signed his name
on the wilted eyes of a magnolia
He covered six raindrops with black silk
His knife cut a cantaloupe in uneven slices
Black was painted over the spots on the dead peacock's tail
From the canopy of his bed hung three skinned chickens
He carefully painted his eyes on his mirror

Paolo pushed his helmet through the blue of a heated ribbon
He tortured the shadows left by crows
The sunflower turned her eyelashes towards his melted gauntlet
A cupid walked on the water in a glass
A river arose in the thighs of the road
On each of his fingers stood a paralyzed bellringer

Francesca's flesh turned the color of sackcloth
A goat nibbled on her fallen pearls
Two disembodied skulls peeped in the broken window
The ashes in the fireplace took off their black robes
A bowl of mango stomped on a stack of nightgowns
The yellow from sweet peppers leaped into her sewing basket
She breathed into the empty skin of an orange
The lute that hung on the wall was plucked by an empty glove
On the floor a severed hand came out of a white cuff
Her tears were the color of old streets
She sewed Paolo's horse to the white wall
Her nameless husband saddled the beach sand
spurred cocinas and sand fleas
chased the cucumber eyes of bobcats
Grafted the pictures of decapitated lizards on his side
His dogs tore the yellow from squashes
The ibis was wounded by his eye glasses
The moon dropped its grapefruit on the sidewalk
Six lawbooks carried him on their shoulders
His bare feet were kissed by blindfolded children
Their mothers blessed their masks
and stuck swords between the eyes of bulls

AN INSIGHT WHILE STANDING
ON A SPOT BY THE HUDSON RIVER
WHERE A BULLDOZER HAD DESTROYED
A GROVE OF ASPEN TREES

They knocked down
the trees
Their ballpoint pens knocked
down the trees
Their wives switched on
the electric lights
pretended the lights
were moons
Their wives stood
on pillows
pretended the pillows
were mountains
Their wives howled
like coyotes
They came home
shot their wives
and turned in their skins
for bounty

ONE'S COUNTRY

It is hard to speak of one's country.
No one knows what it is;
all that has been spoken
should have been unspoken.
The British should never have
built that museum of weapons
and put a plaque
where the Irish bomb exploded,
but should have played recordings
of the tower's ravens.
The country I know is not in the archives,
not in the illusions spoken by retired colonels,
not in the empty words of history books,
but in the shadows,
those unrepeatable dark spots
made on the shore sand by sandpipers.

ON HOWARD FRANKLIN BRIDGE

Hundreds of cars on bridge, stalled,
greyhound track opening.
Three skimmers out for a night flight,
slash openings in the dark water.
On the island reluctantly shoveled from the bay
a row of planks tacked to one another
and a cement mixer that cries like a coyote at the moon.
Now that the herons and terns have been chased away
industry lays its eggs.
The lights inside the condominiums
put their paws on the card players' faces.
The cars will never move, racing forms
propped on steering wheels.
On the other side of the highway fence
a lone sandpiper strolls slowly
down the small strip of moonlit sand
and turns over clam shells.
In each uncovered spot
a door to the earth.

NEL MEZZO DEL CARMIN DI NOSTRA VITA

You go to strange roads to find a space
that built you. The roads never
have been paved, not enough traffic.
On borders a row of statues. Each
has a part missing, a hand, a leg,
or a head. Each has a label, but the name
does not correspond to what is named.
One says, "St. Paul in a trance after
falling from his horse," but actually
it is Naropa sitting on an antelope skin,
although in autumn it could be easily
taken for a Navaho sand painting. Those
who have observed through telescopes
swear it is a clothesline. The road
signs are bizarre. The arrows are bent
backwards and point to where you have come
from. The letters are faded but a faint
outline seems to say, "Private Property.
Keep Off." But not a footmark or tiremark
has even appeared to press down the wild grasses
or disturb the inexplicable pattern of ruts.
Speculation holds the marks made on the sand
were made by herons, raccoons, possums,
armadillos, bobcats, and lizards — as they
were the only visitors ever welcomed. It has been
pointed out that the marks resemble
Egyptian hieroglyphics, or the Hindi text
of Kabir's poems, or the Persian of Rumi's.
It is held by a few that the signs
had no maker, but grew up spontaneously,
unexpectedly, overnight as Australian pines do.
Some say they are not signs at all, but
fallen pine needles. On the edge
near a new housing development, there
is what appears to be a "For Sale" sign.
The numbers are written backwards, in the
handwriting of Leonardo. They are probably

a phone number, or perhaps a secret code.
When a cemetery was removed from the Northern
tip of the island, a journal was found
in one of the graves. An entry said
the "For Sale" sign was put up by a boy
on his way home from school. The boy
did it to please his parents, and the sign
had no meaning or reality beyond
being a gesture to seek praise.
The writer confessed that he was the boy
and asked for forgiveness.
When the sign is examined closely, it can be seen
there are some indecipherable words
written over and behind the numbers,
but this is a different style of writing,
written forward and none of the "t's"
are crossed. It seems to be an ancient calligraphy,
but there is a similarity to the original
in the curves of the vowels. It was as if
written by the same person after an injury
or something that made the hand unsteady.
Many were asked, but none on the island
had ever heard of the writer of the journal.
There were the usual arguments
about the authenticity of the transcriptions
and translations. The journal was written
in mixtures of French, Flemish, Italian,
Latin, German, and Swiss-German. After
the original handwriting in the journal
faded away, a twig with two leaves sprouted
from the binding. No real estate man
ever went near. It was said that the palmettos
and bay bushes were too abundant for anyone
ever to build a tennis court a peep show a jail or
a casino on this fertile region. Its very
density caused it to be denounced or avoided.
Its capacity for growth even created envy
and the public voted to stop the sewer line

NEL MEZZO DEL CARMIN DI NOSTRA VITA

at its borders. Surveyors found it impossible
to make a map. For often they found the palmettos
where the bay bushes were supposed to be. Once
a fund was sought to build a wall and shut
this region off from the rest of the world,
but indifference prevailed. The general concensus
was that no one ever inhabited this place. Some
said it did not exist, or at least there was no
empirical evidence. But someone must have
dug the ditches around it and put up piles
of dirt at all possible entrances. At each
possible entrance there were empty cans
and old sandwich wrappers as if people
out for pleasure had come this far and went no further.
There is no certainty when this debris from over
a thousand picnics had its origin, or will
have its end. It was even suggested
that the ditches were dug to keep the grass
from covering up the evidence of pleasures.
The lighthouse keeper often bored with watching
the complex motion of sea gulls and longing
for a simple motion like the turning of a wheel
often set his telescope on this area. He hoped
he would see an automobile. He longed for
something that could be mathematically analyzed
or mechanically charted. But he never saw
anything that ever made sense to him. Once he
saw a bush start to burn. But there was no cause,
and he looked the other way. He said no human
or any domesticated thing ever frequented this place.
Not even a stray dog. Once when he observed
from a distance the whole place began to look
like some radiant bird, but he surmised
this happened because he had stood too long in the sun.

STARFISH

Benevolent, benevolent beyond all those
who strive and attempt to be bountiful,
benevolent and indifferent starfish,
you know my presence only as a shadow,
a vibration in the absence of light,
a thief of the sun, one who changes
the color of your mind, you know me
as a threat, a danger, an intrusion,
an excresence, a mistake of evolution;
but as I gaze at your orange body
under a thin covering of green water,
you gave me life, a sacred state of consciousness.
I cannot explain you, all biologists have lied,
but starfish, I am transformed by your existence.

AN EVENING IN LJUBLJANA, YUGOSLAVIA

Across the street the sky has red hair
and combs a Siamese cat

A friendly voice is telling me
about clocks wild flowers woodpiles and cathedrals

A stout woman loads a pitchfork of silence on a cart
a girl in blue hoes the rows of quietness

Chickens not confined by commerce to cages
peck the rain from a pile of hay

Old wooden barns arise out of radiant fields
The light becomes a flock of sheep

The moon is covered by hop vines
and brightened by Sljivovica

Stone houses run towards me
and leap into my bones

PAST MARIBOR, YUGOSLAVIAN MOUNTAINS AT SUNSET

The light is a wild flower
that never had
a stem

Its leaves
are the dark glint
of two lovers
on a disappearing road

The petals are colored
river green and waterfall silver

Its pollen
the raw gold
of a rock

Its roots
under the hoof tracks
of cows

A NIGHTINGALE IN ROTHENBURG, GERMANY

A buff
envelope placed in a
yellow
mailbox

A house martin
feeds
young
in a nest on
Rathaus

Behind a half-timbered ochre
and blue plaster
house
the unseen source
of a song

the now
the only eternal

DUTCH LANDSCAPE, NEAR AMSTERDAM

Windmills, red brick houses, cabbages,
artichokes,
        goats, cows, pigs, sheep
black birds in deep grass,
             cherry trees,
rows of trees with thin dark trunks,
and then
a solitary tree
by a ditch of silver water
and in the
tree's aged hand
a green candle
with a flame of rain.

THE HAGUE

The Hague was built out of light,
a crystal light
washed on stones by the wind.
The brooms and their dust
have halos.
In the windows, large and always open,
the light is lace.
The moon never departs
but stays all day in a flower pot.
The avenues leisurely stroll
and lovingly hold the hands of canals.
All houses
are Vermeer paintings
hung on the sky.

A POEM TO VERMEER

You, lucid and secret,
precise and mysterious,
realist and visionary.
You who changed
a girls body
from a thought, a concept,
an allegory, an illusion
into preciousness
and flesh. You always
clothed your figures
and presented the nude
better than Rubens
and his ego imprisonment.
You understood the divinity of woman
better than Bachofen or Neuman.
You who saved the sacred
from its death with the death of angels.
You who found the sacred lived
on the edge of a broom, tacks on a chair,
nails in a wall, the tip of a walking cane,
braid on a cushion, or a neglected shutter.

You understood the language
of interior walls
before Utrillo understood
the language of outside whitewash and plaster.
When you put yourself in a painting
you turned your back
and became unrecognizable
to those who identify
by the obvious and illusory.
You are known
for you are
the wood of the easel,
the book cover,
the fall of the cloth

over a chair,
the fold in a curtain.
You knew
objects exist
not to be owned
but to
create us.

THE OUTSKIRTS OF FLORENCE WERE ALWAYS THERE

You leave the Contessa,
her villa,
    the dark fireplace,

the dark beams
that cross the old ceiling.

    You walk
    down a
    narrow bumpy road,
    each side
    unknown flowers,
    gigantic
    green pods.

Suddenly
a pink wall stands up;
on the pink wall
three shadows,
three washed socks.
You drop into
a day buried
within
and hold
its radiant breath
in your hand.

SWISS ALPS

With eyes I did not know
I had
I look at snow

Higher up
like the shirt
of a formal suit
the river frozen

Nearer
a waterfall stands up
and speaks
from behind
the dark wood
of an ancient barn

Before
a bridge of snow
no one
crosses

Beneath
far below
a slope of wild flowers
that still glow
and grow inwardly

I belong to this mountain

FLORENCE, ITALY

When I came from the darkness,
a mountain tunnel, I noticed
the light wore an old robe,
read manuscripts: misty villas,
misty domes, misty walls, misty towers.

I decided to give the text of my self
to these scholars of light.
The current canon of my years was found
to be a copy of the compiler's life
and referred to someone else.

The light that came out of the olive trees
when the wind upturned their top leaves
confessed each olive tree had a twist all its own,
each interpretation would be biased, based on the twist;
but since my moments were these pale flickering greens
above the darker leaves, and since my body
was the bark and its quest, each exegesis would be correct.

In Florence, the polychrome light, Prato green,
Carrara white, Maremma pink, Giotto's Campanile
rang out its explications, and I understood better
the cryptic passages scribbled on inner pages.

The light from a Ghiberti door
gave my life a gold border;
I became more careful
of careless finger marks.

The head scholar of light, the one
with the most titles, the light of evening
came as the white and green marble
of Santa Maria del Fiore
and wrote notes on a thousand index cards.
Each note said: *He is in love with Florence.*

I REMEMBER GIORGIO DE CHIRICO AS I WALKED DURING NOON DOWN THE VIA DEL QUIRINALE TOWARDS THE VITTORIANO MONUMENT

These
squares
in
Rome
actually
are
hallucinations.

The
realists
painted
illusion.

BOBOLI

The gardens now closed.
I stayed too long
in the Pitti Palace.
I was fascinated
by the gold designs
on ivory doors.

I have become
a connoisseur
of artifical grottos:
Hellbrun, Ludwig's,
and wanted to inspect
Buonlalenti's.

But actually I wanted
to follow Dino Campara
into his *giardino spettrale*,
feel like autumn
in summer.

But too late,
tomorrow
I will climb Assisi
and stand
once more
in the dark
by candles.

I go out
by the overfed dwarf
who sits on a turtle
and stand before
the Pitti's stones.

I feel their brown massive music
creep through my shirt.

THE ROADSIGN SAYS WE ARE NEAR DACHAU

I have been
observing commonplace
people

They never eat
liver
in any form

Have anchovies
removed
from their pizzas

Think Las Vegas
and Miami Beach
are great places

Know the price
and model
of every car

Their children
are land
developers

Their greatest joy
is
killing
animals

We are always
near
Dachau

THE BORGHESE GARDENS

My eyes limped
from shadow to shadow
of the white statues
arranged in a row,

a beheaded stone swan,
trash
in a dry fountain.

Rome is a bare
flowerbed.

By a recess in a wall
surface peeled and speckled
I saw an old woman
feed stray cats:
grey, calico, tabby—
both classical and mackeral.

Rome began to bud.

AT MAINZ, BY THE RHINE RIVER

I look at this grey-brown river, rapid,
boats instead of legends, and think of
long-haired wet girls and a dwarf
who renounced love for the power of gold,
not its glitter.

The road's other side gives me a dove,
a soft grey, almost a black collar, unafraid,
back crossed by stem shadows, strolls from pink roses.

The morning was small farms, frontyard
dark purple roses; lavender, cerulean
pillows air on old stone windows.

My blood still beats with the ancient rhythm
it learned from walking on cobblestone streets
that climb towards a tower and a moon.

I still possess the rainbow colored light
I picked up off the floor
at the Cathedral of Cologne.

LUDWIG II

I became exalted when I saw the island
Ludwig bought to save the trees.

While at Schonburnn I was made happy
when I overheard
that the mayor of Vienna was forced to resign
because he wanted to cut down fifteen trees.

I admired Ludwig when I learned
he dined with his horse.
He found the conversation never as boring
as when he dined with Bismarck
and other practical people.
Ludwig used his brain's right hemisphere,
worshipped Wagner's operas, read good literature,
hated hunters; therefore
he was slandered by the transcribers of his diaries.

My salary will not allow me to live where I want to live,
in a Neuschwanstein, Homenschwangu,
Linderhof, or Herrenchiemsee,
but I can live somewhat like Ludwig
by dining with my Abyssinian cat named Dan Di Lion.

PARIS IN LATE SPRING

What I remember most about Paris

I have already forgotten Maxims
Moulin Rouge Champs Elysées
Tour de Eiffel La Place de la Concorde
the omnipresent movie *Emmanuele*
even the *Maison* de Jean Giraudoux

Still lingering in my memory
are the Africans from French Colonies
who sell on the steps of Sacre Coeur
beads drums other things made in the suburbs

I cannot forget
the lights in tunnels under highways
that change the color of coats
and make everyone look like a corpse

I do recall
the Louvre's Redons and Levy Dhumer's
man with seaweed hair
and his old man in the snow who gripped bamboo

And I remember
Sunday at Notre Dame
the organ played
I was a window
and had a new brain

But what I remember most of all
was a dragonfly's sunlit wing's
holy light
on a dark iron spike

VENICE

Late summer, late summer green water.
Reflections. Swallows always above.
Black and white cat on bank.
Monet and I should have been born in Venice.
We came too late. This gondola plays
an accordian and a guitar. The gondolier sings
about Roma, Firenza, and Napoli, never Venezia.
Rilke came to Venice. He did not want
to hear German spoken. Lived at Palazzo Valmarana.
The brown stains on the peach walls deepen.
The purple pali darken. The empty wine bottle
on a sidewalk table glows. A pair of rubber gloves
that hangs on a clothes line glistens.
I came to Venice because I did not want
to hear anyone speak English. The vaporetti
speak English. The bridges are crowded with
Americans. Although I am in this gondola,
I am in the cage with the canary that sings
from the balcony. Like the canary
I do not sing to those who own me,
those who lean against walls that crumble and sink.
I sing to the stone snails atop
Santa Maria della Salute,
to the Scala dei Giganti's marbles,
to those blue tinted grey bricks
where the pink plaster has fallen,
but most of all,
I sing
to the cross of light
carried on the shoulders of darkness
in San Marco.

AFTER WALKING BY THE STATUE
OF PARACELSUS IN SALZBURG, AUSTRIA

I stand on a bridge
between the old and the new city.
I stand over rapid brown water,
and long for a rhythm,
not the rhythm of the Mirabell flowers,
not the rhythm of the Mirabell trees,
but the rhythm
of the roots
of the wild ferns
that frow from the cracks
in the Mirabell wall.

FROM A ROAD BETWEEN ROME AND MILAN

Flatland vineyards
Upper leaves
wind isolated
move together
Bottom leaves
deeper green
sparkle on
brown goats

A black hat
edge missing
floats
through long field
of sunflowers
towards the forest

An abandoned old
stone house
crumbles
into dark chickens
and flashes

A long sack
dark patches
sun stitched
walks
through wild poppies

Dark sun
Cloud
separated from
other clouds
has a rainbow
all its own

FOAM ON GULF SHORE

FOAM ON GULF SHORE

1. A Glimpse and Premonition

*A transparent woman
of past voices
fills my night.*

— Nicomedes Suaréz-Araúz

Foam on gulf shore
creature
book of the earth
created on the waves' edge by the wind
bubble
alone on brown sand
bubble with shoulders and arms

I also am alone
but my mind
is filled with a crowd
that speaks a language
I must unlearn
I must amputate my mind
this burden
grafted by strangers
on my blood
I must become uninhabited
to inhabit
your body of water

Foam
momentary wind-shaped water
sea born girl
coral colored hair
body of illumination
Aphrodite
Venus
Undine
at low tide among broken sea weed

among the gold berries
that are the ashes of the seas' fires
among the broken fishing lines of drunks
the melancholy corks that never wanted to float
the lead that never wanted to leave the mountain
and the bottles
that advance and retreat

There is a fingersmeared bottle
that hates the artificial flavoring of its contents
but knows without the contents
there would be emptiness and the absence of doorknobs
This bottle is my life
There is another bottle
slime-covered
mud-filled
inside is a dark crab
concealed under the bedsheets of the sun
This is the bottle I want to be

My past has been a card game
played by people who scribbled in chalk
their names on the sidewalk
My rearview mirror wants to forget
what it has passed

Foam
wind-shaped girl
I confront you
and write us
The geometry of your body
my loneliness
The wind makes you irregular
my birth
Your eyes change color
my rapture

I try to explain all this
to the numbers on houses
and find myself bitter

I once sought
the rainbows on your sides
on your waist your hips your breast
buried among the shells of the dead
the conches with collapsed sides
I dug into the ground
and you were gone
You do not remain
as do bleached bones

The colors flicker
over your skin
these colors constantly
changed by the wind
Bubble of rainbows
through whom the earth is seen
if I touch you
you explode
Under my fingers a void
empty sand
I reach with the shadow of my hand

I am the poet who specializes
in loving things
snails spiders mud pelicans pine cones
bark feathers fur and the armadillo's hide
No one could love you
as deeply as I do
but I know so well
the trap of the wind
this prison without walls
bars or a locked door
only an open shore and a vast sky
The wind always blows

I now speak words
whose deeper sounds
are beyond my hearing
I say
I cannot destroy what little I have
this moment of foam
by trying to have more
the whole earth and its hair
I will remain on this shore
where hair fingers legs are born
as long as the wind
will allow you to stay
and write us into a poem

2. Fear and Hesitation

Over the water floats
an oblong pure white cloud
Its shadow an oblong blue
amidst emerald water
Foam
the deep blue of the shadow
wants to be the blue of your eyes
but I must speak the word

I am afraid and silent
I cling to what is not and sustains

A skimmer flies low over the water
His orange bill streaks the water
the streaks he leaves
want to become your blood
but I must speak the word

I listen to the struggle
between the embryo and the fossil

A turnstone upturns a stone
the word under the stone
leaps into my body
I have the word to begin you
The summer legs of the turnstone send a quivering red reflection
across the bubbles that you are
It is the beginning of your lips
Every hair on my arm vibrates

An oyster shell embedded in a black rock
tossed back and forth in your foam
The shell's glow
the beginning of your teeth
A moonshell breaks through the sand

FOAM ON GULF SHORE

leaves a circle of sand on the sand
the circle awakens me to another word
Your hair dangles and seeks a shoulder

The wind blows
The old assumptions return
the true words I have been given
make no sense
I have lost my confidence
and filled with fear
I hear an old woman
speak cruel and false wisdom
I hear my ancestors invite me
to spend my living days in the cemeteries of their words
I cannot abandon the clock and enter time
I see the phosphate plant's smoke
I see rows of cement blocks
tennis courts swimming pools
where once the last terns put their eggs
to hatch words for poems

I now deprived
by the return of civilization
to my body
I am as tight and constricted
as the sea anemone
attached to the whelk shell
cast out of his true home
the cosmic water
onto a smear made by a shoe

I am once more a citizen
an upholder of ruins
a perpetrator of destruction
The blessed vultures no longer
give me instructions
on how to survive among the dead

The holy ibis
no longer teaches me how to fly
As a citizen
I am shut off from all sacred things
crimes and insults multiply in my blood

The wind blows

Let the sea gull drop me on the stone
and crack
this shell my ego
Let me spatter and spread over the earth

Let me
live as the wild flowers
whose white now blazes
out of the pine shadows
whose white is illuminated
by the sun
that found its way
through the pine needles

But foam
I am still lost
because I have an address
cannot wander aimlessly
between the shadow of the osprey
and the shadow of the eagle
I am still hindered and opposed
by the remnants of habitual thinking
that inhabit my body

I am afraid to absorb myself in the sea turtle
to receive words from the sea turtle
to receive words from the tracks of the sea turtle
to receive words from the wrinkled earth that is her nest
I am afraid to absorb myself in the red bellied woodpecker

to receive words from the red bellied woodpecker
that flies inside the dark hole of the white pine
I am afraid to absorb myself in the other
to gather the words I need to create you

The wind blows

As a citizen
I mated my love to my ego
Foam
as a poet
created by animals plants and minerals
I could extend my arm through space
reach inside the moon
take out a bracelet
of hitherto unknown light
to put on your yet unborn arm
and turn your arm of water
into an arm of skin
But what I create becomes another me

The wind blows

Foam
no matter what you become
I must invent you
become abandoned by the crowd
that believes in the familiar and the known
I must touch your hair
become defenseless before those who throw words
I must become abandoned to create you
I will become friends with divine things
with sand fleas coquinas ghost crabs
and all else
that hides underground

I pick up coral
stare into the dark openings
Each opening
has a word to create you
The dark purple threads of the jellyfish
that have touched the coral give me a word
The gold light from the sea worm
that has touched the coral gives me a word
The dark rainbows inside the mussels
that cling to the coral give me a word
The green fields inside the limpits
that caress the coral give me a word
The purple cloud inside the sea hare
the forest on the side of sea slugs
the lamps carried by the squid
the transparency of the baby octopus

I say
let the words leap from everything
let the words leap
from the sand dollar's fur
let the words leap
from the dark spots made by rain on shore sand
let the words leap
from the skeleton exposed by the cracked skin
of the eyeless fish
let the words leap
from the cries of willets
from the white flashes on their wings
from the pink spots
on the cream colored back of the stone crab
from the gold threads
loosened from the hull of the coconut
from the barnacle covered black driftwood
from the hermit crab that has lost his shell
from the horseshoe crab burrowed in mud

let a holy language be born

I witness its birth
I witness
your birth
girl
now girl
no longer foam
I witness our birth

but girl
you are not born naked
you are born
fully grown
and clothed

3. Prelude to Nudity or Death

I touch where your eyes should be
and find tears
It is the sky crying
not your face

Even the distance knows my sorrow
for the empty spaces
we see as blue
can hear the preverbal
expressions of my inner mind
The estranged sky
like all sympathetic things
helpless to act
cries
spreads its iridescence
over the other blue
of your cold eyes
It is the sky's trick to circumvent
my surrender to despair

The closer you come
the more obscure your cold
The more
baffling the flame
that appears as a nail
stuck in your heart
the bleeding is heat
the blood is fear
It is your agony
beneath the chill of your calm clothes
that keeps me warm
It is the struggle against the wind
by the sea oats inside your flesh

that causes me not to freeze
if the wound heals
if you allow a bandage
to cover the drops of red
you immortalize your clothes
to become a monument on our tomb
Let the blood spurt
become our breath
but you still speak
a voice separate from me
say there is no nail
We must obey
the diagram of a star
not the star and the night
You point to your clothes

In the distance
vague shapes in the mist
snowy egrets sit
on the whitened limbs
of fallen trees
In the sky the angular darkness
of a man-of-war bird
The forked tails of the porpoise
sink into the green water
A splash from the dive of a pelican
You have brought me to this landscape

A sun streak across the water
On one side a deep green water
On the other side a strange blue water
a mystic blue
a color unknown before
I first saw your eyes

You girl
who sit on the white sand
the place the dead dry

the dead starfish break
the dead sea urchins crumble
the empty shells bleach
On the white sand above the damp sand
where the dangers of birth reign
the mangrove seeds penetrate the earth

Cold one
the sand has become your snow
You surround yourself with ice
as Brunhilde was surrounded by fire
Your Wotan is your fear
Now that your water
has become your clothes
your covered body
fills my language
with the vocabulary of cannibals
Our words eat the stars
We exchange the clarity of high walls
We dig the grave
for the brown light
that streaks the broken shell
The clothes
must be torn
by your hands
from your body
if we are to be delivered
from being destroyers
if we are to cease
tearing apart the liberty of birds
to cease the burial of the earth
inside our brains

Your clothes a perfect fit
long fingered by the Hebrews and Greeks
A thousand years in each thread
Cloth on which the earth disappears

the old word and not the gulf glitters
Only violence can remove your clothes
But the violence must be your own
Your hands must bleed
There is no other way to your nudity
no other way to our birth
no other way to the creation of the earth
Only your violence
can make us the first cause
a god
a god not imprisoned beyond the skies
but a god to create us

Each knows ourselves
loved by the other
Each knows but we only gaze
I awkward you cold
The ancient order driving you away
the poet seeking you
Although close
in the narrowest of space
we never touch
We depart from the other
and from ourselves
through the exits of the cloth and the wind

4. Desire for Destruction and Revolution

Girl spread out on the white dry sand
Why do you resist me
You say that we must overlook
what the shells and the sand fleas tell us
and believe the paved streets and bridges
I hear the muffled dogs yelp
behind the backyard fences in your brain

Girl without name
I know
as the sun and the sky
in the water of the upturned slipper shell know
that you girl hate the cruelty sanctioned by society
You girl whose eyes flash green blue
as the skink flashes
when he runs across the alien ruts
hate as much as I do
those who entice the hungry fish
to the hook that rips open his jaw
those who put buckshot in the quail's body
Yet you obey them
You want to give yourself to me
but they say no
and you echo their no

A sponge
a mango seed
the bones of moonlight
washed up on the shore by the waves
to celebrate our love
grieve

You still speak their language
that is not our language
but inwardly

you have another language
you share a common tongue
with the prickly pear and the sea plum

You who
belong to the sand dunes
not buildings
who belong
to the pathless borders of wild beaches
not hallways
you who recognize the lies
that people daily exchange as truth
refuse to bloodstain your hands
by tearing off your clothes

I spoke you
to overcome them
I spoke you
to save the sting ray
from their spear guns
to let the brown backs of the sting rays
flash gold through the green

Girl without name
I beg you to rebel
disobey
so that I can disobey
Girl
listen to me
Girl
my possible self
Girl
my possible poem
Girl
strip yourself naked
beside the sea oats
Hurry

hurry
for soon
there will be no sea oats
Soon
only condominiums
only spiked condoms
only tennis courts
only vibrators
only inflatable whores of rubber
only masturbation machines
Hurry girl
strip off your clothes
before the sea oats disappear
for when the sea oats disappear
love disappears

You say I should not talk this way
You say I should not say these things
I say
your obedience
sanctions the diseased social order
that sanctions the spear gun
I say to you
if you had seen
the bloody sting ray
dying on the shore
if you had seen the blood
spurt from her breast
If you had seen this sting ray
killed for human pleasure
If you had seen
the bloody sting ray
you would shout to me
disobey
disobey everything they believe in
you would shout
burn their cities

Burn their cities

You would pray for a hurricane
You would have prayed to the ocean
to flood the shore
wash away the foundations
of their murderous condominiums

I see
girl
my rage
has made you more afraid
you avert your eyes
you become more confused
you look at the pictures
of your ancestors
and see they have no faces
you pick up a history book
washed in by the tide
and see the pages are blank

But you still obey

I regret I ever met you
I feel degraded that I loved you

You start to reach towards me
but you turn your back
run away
towards the construction
site
and its bulldozers

5. *Alone on a Shoreline*

The cormorant's tail splashes the water
His dark body arises in flight
His shadow crosses the empty space
where you
girl without name
once were
A darkness fills the dint
your body made on the sand

The egret flies
the water drops
off the yellow feet
the drops disappear
His shadow has the shape
of your sleeve

I look at the red streaks
down the center of green sandspurs
but since you are gone
the red does not speak
The sand in the bottom
of the upturned buttercup shell
does not speak
The algae around the edges
of the whelk eggcase are silent
The water that spurts from the clams
the water that spurts from the oyster
says nothing

Only smoke knows me
Smoke from burning autumn leaves
know me
calls me
by name
my name

that always seems strange
when I hear
smoke say it

I do not want to hear my name

I am desperate
I know I am foolish
but I want
you
I want you more than I ever wanted anyone
I want you
I want to hold you close and know distance
I want to forget infinity
and caress all the sorrows and terrors
of the finite
I want to feel your warmth against my flesh
and know
all the unicorns and cobras of despair

Let me be remade by mistakes
errors
disobedience and disloyalty
by the orchids of uncertainty
that sprout from between mosses on oak branches
Let me predate the stars

Come come
come
like the living light from a dead star
come
like limestone like coral
come
from the death of what was once
tender and fragile
what closed its eyes and trembled
what was ardent and afraid
Come

I do not want to hear what is called wisdom
the dead old man in the wilted rose bushes
I do not want to pretend I know what I see in mirrors
I am tired of living in a dull land
among the nests of hungry costumes

I want you
you who are afraid of the signboards' tongues
afraid of
the missing eye under the black eye patch
you
who have refused to look down
when the shells looked up
I want you
I want the little I can have of you
I want
to expose myself to the hurricane of limitations
I want to suffer
as the shadow suffers
the shadow that knows it has no source
the shadow
that can never leave or cross the road

I want to live
as if destiny never distorted me
to live the life
that I did not want to live
I want to live
like the moon that is barbed with the cry of the panther
like algae on ponds
like lightning behind spider webs
like burrows like caves
like subterranean suns

I know the future is almost gone
death is near
There is only a little time
to seek the impossible solution

Come come
Come
like the living light from a dead star
come
like limestone like coral
come
from the death of what was once
tender and fragile
what closed its eyes and trembled
what was ardent and afraid
Come

The wind blows

You
girl without name
you come out from the sea oats
walk towards me
Your hands bleed
I see the last of your scant clothing is gone

6. *The Poem and Exile*

Girl
now naked
still unnamed
prepare to be named

You were foam
a shape of water
The voices of the earth
created my voice
to speak you into a girl
I saw you I spoke
stand apart from me
and run away
to return
with bloody hands

You tore
off the deceptions
that were your clothes

Naked
you became translucent
to magnify
each sand grain
and the light
in the center of the sand grain
the light
the color of the voice of the crow

Now I must name you
Shall I name you
after one of Mallarme's mysterious women
Shall I call you
the daughter of Douve
or Dupin's naked girl

André Breton's Nadja
If the girls in Delvaux's paintings
had names
I could give you one of their names
Delvaux painted the "End of the World"
I could name you the "End of the World"
Éluard wrote a poem for Delvaux
called "Exile"
I could name you "Exile"

I name you
Exile

For the wind demands your exile
to be turned as pages in other hands
hands that can never love you as my hands have
my hands that touched you before you were born

The wind blows
Now named
you must depart forever from me
When separated
we will find consolaton
that we once walked hand in hand
saw the ghost crab pause
from his rush across white sand
to let us touch his back
Consolation
that we stopped by barnacled black wood
watched the greens and blues of the water
become brown and gold with the backs
of hundreds and hundreds of sting rays
that greeted us as one of them

We have the consolation
that we now hate
the clothes and the words

that delayed the consummation of our love
We have the consolation
that we overcame the language given us
the language that stays apart from things
the language that dements and destroys

Now you say
you do not want
consolations
you want us to stay together
If as poem
you must depart from me
you want to leap
back through my side
stay unborn in my body
you want your water
and your salt
to redden
and become my blood
You want to flow through me forever

The wind blows

We look at each other
as Adam and Eve
looked at each other
when the gate was shut
and the angel
drew from the scabbard
his sword of fire

The wind blows

Let us stare
before you go
at where we are
this space that now predates the social order

We who
in the breath of the porpoise
are anterior to society
We in the dive of the nighthawk
are prexistent to crime

Exile
only I
a poet who specializes in loving things
can love you
But we wasted so much time
you were ashamed to have blood on your hands
it took so long for you
to tear off the deceptions
that were your clothes
when we finally became real and pure bodies
only a little time was left

Exile
do not cry
I cannot stand to watch
the girl I love cry
Stop those tears
The tears mar the beauty
of your bluegreen eyes
a strange bluegreen
A bluegreen seen only be me once before
the bluegreen
of snow shadows in the Dolomites
a strange color
found in this place of intense cold

We wasted so much time

7. The Shore Revisited

Therefore the Love which us doth bind
But Fate so enviously debarrs,
Is the Conjunction of the Mind,
And Opposition of the Stars.
— Andrew Marvell

Things have changed now
There is more pain
Loneliness no longer
can be conquered by illusions
Death is much closer
I despise what I told you then I believe
Things have changed
Now I want you
you whom I refused
You who tried to kill yourself with the wind
because I was afraid to drown
Now I want you
I want to give you
what no one else would have
what the most intimate refused
I want to give you
the secret message
from my unknown self
I thought I was alive
when I lied to you
I even believed it then
but I was not even born
I can say that this time
birth was much worse
Much worse
for I knew so well
where I was
into what I was being born

This time
I really cried
not the baby's surprise
but deeper tears
At this birth
there were no parents
No one
Only a desire
A desire
for what I can never have
A desire
that seems more foolish this time
A desire for someone to whom I can give
the secret message
of my unknown self
This message
I am too awkward to speak
and if I did
I could not understand
You are the only one I know
that would even tolerate its existence
The rest always say
it makes them afraid
or they make it mean
what it does not mean

I sent you away then
and now that
you have returned
in another form
I know I am helpless
a victim of the wind
now that you are here
I will send you away again

ABOUT THE AUTHOR

DUANE LOCKE was born in 1921 on a farm near Vienna, Georgia. His undergraduate work at the University of Florida led to his Masters studies on John Keats and set the foundation for his Doctoral thesis on the poetry of John Donne and Andrew Marvell. He received a Ph.D. in English Renaissance Literature in 1958 and was Professor of English and Poet in Residence at the University of Tampa for over twenty years. At the University of Tampa, he edited three critically acclaimed journals of poetry, *Poetry Review* (1964-1971), *UT Review* (1972-1982), and *Abatis* (1983-1986). He taught courses on every period of poetry ranging from Old English to contemporary, with a concentration in contemporary European and Latin American poetry.

Locke's poems have appeared in such journals as *American Poetry Review, The Nation, The Literary Review, Kansas Quarterly, Black Moon, Ann Arbor Review* and *The Bitter Oleander* to name but a few. At present count he has had over 6,000 poems published in both print and more currently e-zine formats. He is the author of fifteen books of poetry: *From the Bottom of the Sea* (1968), *Inland Oceans* (1968), *Dead Cities* (1969), *The Submerged Fern in the Waistline of Solitude* (1969), *Rainbows Under Boards* (1969), *The Word* (1974), *Immanentist Sutras* (1975), *Starfish Manuscript* (1976), *Various Lights* (1976), *Foam on Gulf Shore* (1978), *Poems of Duane Locke* (1986), *Whoever Raises the Question of Representation in Our Time* (1992), *Watching Wisteria* (1995), and *Yang Chus Poems* (2009). He also has three e-books all published in 2002: *The Squid's Dark Ink* (Ze Books), *From a Tiny Room* (Otos Books, Spain), and *The Death of Daphne* (4*9*1). He has also been anthologized in *Southern Writing in the Sixties* (1968), *The Living Underground* (1969), *This Generation* (1970), *I Am Talking About Revolution* (1973), *The Immanentist Anthology: Art of the Superconscious* (1973), *Mantras* (1973), *Contemporary Southern Poetry* (1978) and *Ghost Dance Anthology* (1994). His honors include the Edna St. Vincent Millay Prize for best sonnet written in that year, the Charles Agnoff Award for best poem in a literary review, and the Walt Whitman Award bestowed upon him by the Poetry Society of America.

THE BITTER OLEANDER
Library of Poetry

BITTER OLEANDER
P R E S S

Torn Apart by Joyce Mansour *—translated by Serge Gavronsky*	$14.00
Children of the Quadrilateral by Benjamin Péret *—translated by Jane Barnard & Albert Frank Moritz*	$14.00
Edible Amazonia by Nicomedes Suárez-Araúz *—translated by Steven Ford Brown*	$11.00
A Cage of Transparent Words by Alberto Blanco *—a bilingual edition showcasing multiple translators—*	$20.00
Afterglow/Tras el rayo by Alberto Blanco *—translated by Jennifer Rathbun*	$21.00
Of Flies and Monkeys/De singes et de mouches by Jacques Dupin *—translated by John Taylor*	$24.00
The Moon Rises in the Rattlesnake's Mouth by Silvia Scheibli	$ 6.00
Half-Said by Paul B. Roth	$10.00
Cadenzas by Needlelight by Paul B. Roth	$16.00
On Carbon-Dating Hunger by Anthony Seidman	$14.00
Festival of Stone by Steve Barfield	$12.00
Infinite Days by Alan Britt	$16.00
Teaching Bones to Fly by Christine Boyka Kluge	$14.00
Travel Over Water by Ye Chun	$14.00
Where Thirsts Intersect by Anthony Seidman	$16.00
Vermilion by Alan Britt	$16.00
Stirring the Mirror by Christine Boyka Kluge	$16.00
Gold Carp Jack Fruit Mirrors by George Kalamaras	$18.00
Van Gogh in Poems by Carol Dine	$21.00
Giving Way by Shawn Fawson	$16.00
If Night is Falling by John Taylor	$16.00
Duane Locke: The First Decade (1968-1978) by Duane Locke	$25.00

All back issues and single copies of *The Bitter Oleander* are available for $10.00
For more information, contact us at info@bitteroleander.com
or visit us
www.bitteroleander.com